KEEPING UP IN A DOWN ECONOMY

WHAT THE BEST COMPANIES DO TO GET RESULTS IN TOUGH TIMES

BOB NELSON, Ph.D.

PRAGMATIC PUBLICATIONS
SAN DIEGO, CALIFORNIA

ISBN-13: 978-0-6153-0661-2

Cover design by Leigh Anne Ference-Kaemmer
Interior design and layout by Nick Swisher

Pragmatic Publications is an imprint of Nelson Motivation, Inc.

**For information about additional products and services, including
speaking and consulting, please contact:**

Nelson Motivation, Inc.
P.O. Box 500872
San Diego, CA 92150-0872
1-800-575-5521 or 858-673-0690
www.nelson-motivation.com

You can contact Bob Nelson directly via email at:
BobRewards@aol.com

To register for Bob's email updates visit: www.nelson-motivation.com

Bulk copies of this book are available from the above address
at the below discounted prices:

1 to 9 copies = $14.95 ea.
10 to 24 copies = 25% discount ($11.21 ea.)
25 to 499 copies = 40% discount ($8.97 ea.)
500 to 999 copies = 50% discount ($7.48 ea.)
1000+ copies = 55% discount ($6.73 ea.)

First printing: August 2009
Manufactured in the USA

ACKNOWLEDGEMENTS

I wanted to thank Lauren Marino, Executive Editor at Penguin who first suggested this project to me, Jeanie Casison-Tanisiri who provided research for the project, Austin Becker who provided research and formatting assistance, Anne Helliker who helped with the initial draft of the manuscript, Jennifer Wallick who helped to edit, develop and format the manuscript, Danny Nelson who helped proofread the manuscript, Leigh Anne Ference-Kaemmer for the cover design and Nick Swisher for the research, development, editing, design and all aspects of the production of this book.

I would also like to thank Robert Half International for granting permission to use "The Most Common Mistakes Managers Make in an Uncertain Economy" that you will find dispersed throughout this book.

PREFACE

An economic recession is a scary thing. Headlines in the news portray a persistent gloom that sinks into the psyche of all employees. Glimmers of hope for improvement in the economy are quickly squelched by the negativity of the next economic indicator. Yet the real toll of the recession is the impact it has on everyday people: those that have lost their jobs, benefits or wages, as well as those who are concerned about losing these things, which is most everybody else.

In this book, I focus on the positive things that can be done with employees in any work environment to impact an organization's success during difficult times. I derived these suggestions from some of the most validated principles of performance management combined with my own primary research as to what most motivates today's employees to be fully engaged where they work. All suggestions are supported with current real-life examples from named companies.

The driver of a car never gets car sick. It's always the person in the back seat who can't control the situation and ends up being stuck for the ride. So it is true that the victim of hard times often feels powerless in the face of overwhelming negative circumstances. As much as possible we need to show employees how they can make a difference in clear and direct ways that can impact their jobs and help the organization.

There are many circumstances managers can not control, but many more that they can directly impact in positive ways. By focusing on those things that can be controlled, managers can help buffer employees from the negative impact of the economy, as well as help channel employee energies to achieve better results. While none of us can change the economy, all of us can control our reaction to poor economic times and focus our efforts in specific ways that can have a positive impact where we work. In so doing, we can create a more positive and productive work environment that will help your company thrive in challenging times.

There is a fine line of difference between stress and excitement. Negative circumstances you can't control lead to stress; negative circumstances you can control are opportunities for excitement. Managers can help employees perceive negative circumstances in positive ways. They have the power to inspire employees to see the opportunities that exist and to encourage and support them in making the most of these opportunities.

Research tells us that the best leaders are positive and forward-looking, especially in difficult times. My hope is that this book will serve as a starting point for discussion and action as to what you and your employees can do to make a difference now, and in the process create positive changes from which you can all directly benefit.

—Bob Nelson
San Diego, California

CONTENTS

KEEPING UP IN A DOWN ECONOMY

WHAT THE BEST COMPANIES DO TO GET RESULTS IN TOUGH TIMES

INTRODUCTION

Keeping Up in a Down Economy

- ◈ What We Can Learn From Past Recessions
- ◈ The Impact on Employee Morale
- ◈ Simple Actions Can Make a Difference
- ◈ Combating the 'You Should Just Be Happy You Still Have a Job' Syndrome
- ◈ What Follows in This Book

W e are in an economic downturn that is deeper and more damaging to the American economy than anything experienced since the 1930s. Recent research conducted by Kenneth Rogoff, a Harvard economics professor, concluded that the current economic crisis will not recover until at least 2011. While the economy will one day surely turn for the better, government economists believe that day may be several years away and that conditions will get worse before they get better. In the meantime, to thrive— or even just to survive—company owners, executives, managers and employees must take action now to help ensure their success and to be able to make it to better times.

By focusing on the right things now, management in any company can make a marked difference in its ability to create more positive circumstances for its employees that allows the organization to compete more effectively. Managers can do this by motivating their employees to achieve focused, revised goals that touch all aspects of the business from innovation and cost-cutting ideas, to process improvement and enhanced customer service, to strategies for enhancing sales, referrals and follow on services.

While this focus may seem like good management practice that companies should already be doing, these basics are even more critical in tough times and can make the difference between success and failure for many organizations today.

Quantum Workplace, a company that tracks employee engagement scores of over 1.5 million employees within 5,000 companies nationwide, has found that 66 percent of the firms they studied saw a decrease in employee engagement in a recent year that seemed to be in direct response to the negative circumstances of the recessionary economy.

Common Mistake #1
Waiting for an economic turnaround to make changes.

Putting business decisions on hold too long takes a toll on your bottom line. If you have a good idea, don't wait for a recovery to implement it. You'll get a head start on the competition by making your move now.

A comparison of those employers that had higher engagement scores with those whose scores had dropped revealed five key differentiators, all of which will be addressed in this book: 1) Setting a clear, compelling direction that empowers each employee, 2) Open and honest communication, 3) Continued focus on career growth and development, 4) Recognizing and rewarding high performance, and

5) Continued employee benefits that demonstrate a strong commitment to employee well-being.

"Employers can significantly influence, if not control, how motivated and satisfied their employees are," says Greg Harris, president of the firm. "A more engaged workforce can act as insulation, a buffer if you will, from the effects of the economic downturn," concludes Mark D. Hirschfeld, principal of Golden-rod Consulting, Inc.

What We Can Learn From Past Recessions

Management taking positive actions in challenging times to obtain positive results is a proven strategy of today's most successful companies, some of which either began or grew substantially during recessions and/or depressions. For example, General Electric started during the panic of 1873 (i.e., "The Long Depression"), a time when Andrew Carnegie also launched his very first steel mill. Carnegie had the foresight to recognize that lower construction costs would allow him to build his dream with little money, a move that ultimately secured him the title as the world's richest man.

Disney started during the post-war recession of 1923-24 and the Great Depression served as a great "incubator" for creativity for that company. Moreover, in addition to GE and Disney, Procter & Gamble, Kellogg, nearly every airline, and Chevrolet all bucked the business trend of the times and actually expanded during the Depression. And, near the end of the Depression, two men took a leap of faith and built a computer company from the ground up in a garage. In the subsequent decades, Bill Hewlett and Dave Packard drove their company, Hewlett-Packard, to be one of the most recognized names in the computing business.

Here are some more recent examples of successful companies that blossomed in challenging times:

- Microsoft was founded during the oil crisis in the mid-1970s.

- At the height of the recession in the early 1980s, IBM led the crusade to introduce the personal computer that would become a milestone for the company and the industry.

- During the 1991 recession, California-based semiconductor company Intel Corporation initiated its "Intel Inside" marketing and branding campaign, and emerged a household name. Before that, it was an anonymous microprocessor supplier. Now, we think of Intel as a brand and we want an Intel chip inside our computer. Since then, Intel has rarely retrenched and consistently made investments during recessions.

- During the 2002 recession, American discount retailer WalMart pushed its "Everyday low prices" slogan. This year, it has launched "Save money, live better." WalMart, known for its low prices, doesn't mind recessions because most everyone looks for better bargains during tight times. In the last two recessions, they took advantage of this fact to position the company strategically.

- When the big car companies were busy laying off workers from 2000 to 2003, Toyota expanded operations, and emerged with a higher market share. During that time, it shut down a plant in Turkey for 10 months, but kept all its workers and trained them. When the plant reopened, it went on to have some of the highest productivity and quality ratings at any Toyota plant globally. Toyota promised that for 2009 it is not going to lay off any of its 4,500 or so U.S.-based employees. Instead, they are shutting down plants for three months and training workers in new techniques and new models.

- In 2008, senior managers at Hewlett-Packard significantly reduced costs, rid themselves of businesses that were no longer profitable and turned all of their attention to the historic strengths of the company. The result? The company not only survived, but they also managed to report profits while competitors did not.

- JPMorgan Chase management made sweeping changes in preparation for tough times ahead and, as a result, cleaned up the bank's balance sheet, placing them several steps ahead of rival banks who crumbled in the resulting financial crisis.

- At a time when everyone else seems to be cutting back or retrenching, AT&T recently announced the $1.2 billion purchase of two additional companies in an aggressive signal that they were not going to let the current downturn prevent them from growing.

In the most recent tumultuous financial environment, these companies not only managed to survive, they continue as recognized industry leaders. Each company took an approach of deciding to do things differently, and successfully communicated and implemented that approach with their employees. Understanding and knowing the consumer mindset was imperative, as was looking for opportunities to excel in challenging times. For some organizations, preparation was the key. It's one thing to have a grasp of performance when things are going smoothly, but it's those companies that have the wherewithal to prepare for the worst of times, and have a plan for navigating through those times, that emerge as the true success stories.

The Impact on Employee Morale

Recessionary times bring more stress, anxiety and fear to all employees, which, if left unchecked, creates a negative work environment that leads to declining morale, eroding trust and loss of productivity for the company. Even before the latest recession, 40 percent of today's employees reported that their jobs were very or extremely stressful, with 25 percent saying their jobs were their #1 stressor in their lives. Sixty percent of employees felt pressure to work too much, and 85 percent reported feeling overworked and under appreciated.

With the onset of the recession, not only are employees worried about the stability of their jobs, they are also concerned about their personal finances and future. Stress wreaks havoc on the body and manifests itself in ways that are often not even evident to the person enduring the symptoms. Regardless, the result at work is almost always a decrease in productivity and an increase in absenteeism. Long hours, lack of support and poor communication are all contributing factors to stress among employees, not the least of which is poor morale.

In early 2009, Accountemps released survey results about the impact of various business practices on employee morale. The survey results were based on interviews with close to 1,500 CFOs throughout the United States who were asked the following question: Which of the following has the most negative impact on employee morale?

- 33 percent cited a lack of honest communication

- 19 percent cited a failure to recognize employee achievements

- 17 percent cited micro-managing employees

- 16 percent cited excessive workload for extended periods

- 14 percent cited fear of job loss

For far too many Americans, getting up and going to work is becoming more difficult. From what we read in the morning newspapers to what we learn online or see on the evening news, the economic outlook is grim. Constant news of the dire state of the world economy creates pessimism and fear in employees. In addition, many workers know former co-workers, family members and friends who have been laid off. As such, keeping a positive outlook is almost impossible for many employees. Fears of layoffs and disappointing reductions in salaries and benefits occupy the minds of all employees. People are struggling at home with how to adjust to personal economic setbacks, and they are paralyzed with fear and uncertainties at work. All of these anxieties and pressures make for unhappy, stressed employees and an unproductive workplace.

It's a natural tendency for anyone facing difficult times to feel hurt and threatened. As a result, employees can become withdrawn, fearful, and myopic. Unfortunately, this reaction tends to perpetuate the original circumstances, causing an entirely new set of concerns, enhanced fears, and negative reactions that can further worsen the situation. According to Peter Capelli, a professor of management at Wharton, "Workers in a downturn can get so nervous that they just freeze up and aren't able to do good work, especially if they're afraid of being laid off and it's not clear what the standards are." The key, then, is to motivate your workers towards improved performance, and not to paralyze them with fear.

Simple Actions Can Make a Difference

Many companies, especially those who have weathered previous recessions or depressions, have come up with practical, simple and inexpensive ways to keep employees inspired and their businesses above water. Take a look at some of the low-cost, morale-boosting ideas that have recently worked for companies across America:

- One company offered "redeployments" to unrelated positions instead of layoffs.

- One firm established a 24-hour "news desk" on its company Intranet that was constantly updated with the latest company news for its employees to check.

- A number of organizations allowed their employees (not just management) to run cost-cutting programs.

- One company cut back operating hours and shifted all employees to a four-day work week while others allowed more flexible work schedules for their employees.

- Many organizations scheduled more team-building activities, but they also allowed employees to decide which team-building activities they would like do (not everyone enjoys paintball after all).

- One bank created an Asset Relief Program in which all employees, not just upper management, were asked how to increase business and help address slumping profits.

- Many organizations encouraged managers to write sincere, handwritten thank-you notes to their employees rather than giving cash.

- Many companies gave employees additional time off in lieu of pay increases or bonuses.

- One large company established a monthly "Take Your Dog to Work Day."

- Another company established a monthly "Family Day" in which workers were encouraged to bring their family in for the day.

- One company replaced expensive catered lunches with brown bag lunches prepared by managers.

- A few companies got creative and recycled employee trophies as new awards.

- One firm allowed its employees to bank and share vacation time.

- To lessen economic anxiety, a few companies created money management courses for their employees to take.

- Other firms encouraged their employees to take their vacation time and maintain a better work-life balance in their lives.

- To get their employees to stop thinking about the doom-and-gloom in the news, one company in the Northeast allowed their employees to organize fundraisers for those less fortunate than themselves.

- Some companies allowed faith-based groups, diversity groups, and book clubs to form.

These are just some of the simple, useable ideas that you can start to have work for you and your employees to help make a difference today. Many more ideas and techniques will follow that can be weaved into your daily practices and the fabric of your company's culture.

Combating the 'You Should Just Be Happy You Still Have a Job' Syndrome

One of the worst mistakes managers today can make is to assume that recognizing their workers is not as important now as when unemployment is low. Managers can't assume that employees should simply be thankful for having a job and so don't need to be further motivated or encouraged to be productive. While there is no doubt that most employees who have survived a layoff are indeed thankful for their job, this feeling will hardly be enough to engage them to new heights during a time when their focused efforts are most needed. From strong communication programs to remembering to say thank you, there are many ways to motivate employees and help them endure the changes that come with a down economy.

Common Mistake #2
Feeling people are lucky just to have a job.

This assumption is based on the belief that when the economy is weak people feel fortunate to have a stable position, even if it's not their ideal job. While this may be true in some cases, remember that your most talented employees always have options. Good people are marketable in any economy, and you want your best performers to stay with you for the long term.

What Follows in This Book

Chapter 1, "Create a Clear & Compelling Direction," looks at ways you can create more realistic goals for your group or organization. Since all performance starts with clear goals and expectations, revising existing goals and setting new expectations is critical in a quickly changing economic climate. To help better achieve those goals, the next four chapters address the top categories of motivation reported by today's employees and hence offer some of the most powerful ways to fully engage employees in any work setting today.

Chapter 2, "Direct, Open & Honest Communication," is important during challenging times and represents the top-reported employee motivator necessary for any employee to do a good job at work. Everyone needs to have answers to their questions and adequate information, not just about their jobs, but also about what's going on in other parts of the organization, new products and services and the organization's strategies for success.

Chapter 3, "Involve Employees & Encourage Initiative," seeks to explicitly give employees permission to act in the organization's behalf whether that is through idea suggestions, problem solving, exceptional customer service, or a host of other possibilities.

Chapter 4, "Increase Employee Autonomy, Flexibility & Support," will show you how to grant employees permission to further pursue and develop their ideas into practical solutions for the organization. It gives every employee a greater say in their own job and how best to accomplish the tasks and responsibilities they are charged with achieving.

Chapter 5, "Continued Focus on Career Growth & Development," shows how employees can make the most of opportunities that arise from the constantly changing demands of the times. Most learning and development occurs on the job in the work that employees are encouraged to do on a daily basis.

Chapter 6, "Recognize & Reward High Performance," represents the most significant driver of desired behavior and performance for any manager and any organization. Special attention is given to how you can focus on low- and no-cost forms of recognition that are especially meaningful in challenging times.

Most employees are motivated to do a good job where they work. I've yet to meet an employee who got up in the morning and hoped to make a mess of things at work! Employees want to help the organization as best they can to be successful, but they can't do this in a vacuum. Managers need to provide leadership and support to help create the context for their employees' success. This book provides that context for managers to use with their employees.

CHAPTER 1

Create a Clear & Compelling Direction

- ❖ What's Working & What's Not
- ❖ Revised Goals & Renewed Focus
- ❖ Guidelines for Effective Goal Setting
- ❖ Provide Frequent Feedback to Help Employees Stay on Track
- ❖ Link Goals to Financial Rewards
- ❖ Summary

The starting point of any organizational change is with a clear and compelling vision for the organization. If employees are not inspired by what the organization is trying to do, it will be more difficult for them to have the motivation and direction to succeed—especially in tough times. Frances Hesselbein, president of the Leader-to-Leader Foundation, once put it this way: "No matter what business you're in, everyone in the organization needs to know why." Do a reality check and ask employees what the mission and purpose of the organization is. If you get a different answer from each person you ask, it's a good indication that things have drifted or perhaps have not been clear for some time. Use this opportunity to revisit the purpose of your business group or function. Management guru Peter Drucker used to advocate that management ask three questions: 1) What is our business? 2) Who is our customer? 2) What does our customer consider value? In this way, Drucker helped connect what organizations were trying to achieve with their customers in the marketplace.

Clarifying one's vision is a useful starting point for deciding what is most important for the organization (or department) to focus on to be successful.

Common Mistake #3
Ignoring the higher purpose.

What motivates you and your staff to come to work every day? It's probably not to see how much profit you can build for the company. Think about the bigger picture: Does your firm provide products or services that make life or work easier, safer or more enjoyable for your clients or customers? Is your company involved in philanthropic efforts? Know your organization's higher purpose and be sure your team members do too.

The result needs to be a compelling purpose that can inspire everyone. "A vision is not just a picture of what could be, it is an appeal to our better selves, a call to become something more," says Harvard professor Rosabeth Moss Kanter. From that vision you can shape your "unique competitive advantages," that is, those aspects that you have to offer your customers that your competition does not. These advantages represent your strengths in the marketplace that you most need to capitalize on to be successful. In changing times, the unique advantages you have to offer and the needs of your customers can shift drastically, so it makes sense to look at this frequently.

Exelon Focuses on Vision and Strategic Direction

Exelon, one of the nation's largest power generation and distribution companies, makes an extra effort to develop organizational culture and positive attitudes. First, they have created a vision document which outlines goals and values. Then, they have a strategic direction document which exists to protect company values and to grow long-term value.

These two documents are the foundation of everything Exelon does. From goal setting to business decisions, the company relies upon the contents of these documents for guidance. This is also how they measure their employees in terms of performance, potential and forward thinking.

What's Working & What's Not

Once you have clarified your vision for your group, analyze what is currently working, and what is not, for the business. Established customers may be cutting back on using the services of your firm, but what new clients have recently started to invest with you? What do those new clients have in common and how can you approach similar clients in the marketplace? Changing times call for changing strategies to meet your company's goals. Engage employees to determine what is working and what is not.

For example, one computer equipment and software company based in San Diego saw its future orders drop significantly. Its sales representatives reported that customer capital budgets were being frozen and customers no longer had the budget to purchase capital equipment. The firm's business model required that its customers purchase both hardware and software, which they would completely own, and then pay ongoing maintenance fees to have the firm service both the equipment and the software that ran that equipment.

The firm did a layoff of about 10 percent of its employees and froze salaries, but knew that was just

Common Mistake #4
Making work 'mission impossible'.

Layoffs and budget cuts may mean one person is doing the job of two, or even three, people. If this is the case, decide which duties are mission-critical, and focus on those. Delegate remaining tasks, bringing in temporary professionals if necessary, or put these items on hold. This will help you avoid overwhelming your staff or setting them up for failure.

Common Mistake #5
Playing it safe.

Tried-and-true formulas and "safe" creative expression can be alluring in uncertain times because they're, well, safe. But "boring" never got any business very far. Take calculated risks and break new ground, or you'll quickly lose your competitive edge.

a short-term fix for the projected declining cash flow. More importantly, top management got together with the firm's sales representatives and brainstormed what could be done to address the situation and also what the competition was doing in response to the situation. As a result, revised strategies were launched, which included:

• A change in the pricing model to include new options for payment, for example, a "per use" leasing payment model, which didn't require the customer to make an expensive up front purchase of equipment.

• A new, software-only solution that for the first time allowed customers to run needed applications on existing computers they owned or equipment they wanted to purchase from other vendors.

• New financing options in which the company started financing the purchase of their equipment. This allowed clients to be able to begin using the company's product without having to initially tap into resources from their capital budget.

• Targeted new markets such as the Federal government (which had more available funds), which the company had never before targeted.

All of these changes required everyone in the organization to help think through implications for the business and make adjustments accordingly. The result was that the firm was able to get new clients who took them up on their

Common Mistake #6
Not considering the economy's effect on customers.

Uncertain economic times can be both a bane and a boon for businesses. Researching and understanding customers' changing ideas about what they consider "worth the money" can help firms better tailor their products and services to the times.

new offerings such as the ability to lease versus purchase the company's equipment, while they continued to service the changing needs of their existing clients.

Some of the strategies employed are longer term and hence are still being developed, but overall the approach has helped the firm to generate new sales revenue from new clients in a difficult financial time.

Home Depot Revises Goals and Retains Bonuses

When Home Depot was forced to close locations and cut jobs at their corporate headquarters, CEO Frank Blake didn't waste any time restoring morale and revising goals. His immediate action was to extend the restricted stock grants for all store managers, then he reviewed the sales targets for hourly employees. Because annual bonuses are triggered by sales and profit results, he lowered the targets. Even with lower targets, achieving them was difficult in this economy, but the result was the highest percentage in Home Depot's history of hourly employees receiving bonuses.

Reducing bonus targets did not mean that employees had to work less, or put forth little effort. In fact, it gave them an added incentive to work that much harder. By revising the goals, employees were shown that the company was keeping their best interest in mind. Had sales goals remained the same, the likelihood of employees reaching their targets would have been next to impossible, which, in turn, could have caused them to simply give up and assume an attitude of "why bother?"

The move by Home Depot's CEO ensured that employees would not throw up their hands, but instead instilled motivation and hard work. He also sent employees a message that just because the company was struggling did not mean that corners would be cut in terms of their compensation. Home Depot still had to pay bonuses, but as a result they developed employees who were committed to helping the company sustain sales and profits.

Revised Goals and Renewed Focus

You've set your vision and you've analyzed what's working and what's not for your organization, now it's time to set goals. In tough times, managers need to prioritize and revaluate existing company and employee goals—ideally with the individuals most responsible for attaining them—and ensure they are focused on what matters most to the company and its customers. In economic down times, most company's goals shift to concentrate on how they plan to revise their way of doing things to save money, be more efficient and keep up with, or ahead of, the competition. Employees need to feel a sense of control over their position within the company and be reassured that managers have control over the bigger picture. When profits are down, it's time to review company-wide goals as well as the goals of each individual employee. Doing so provides employees with a greater sense of direction and control, and ensures that everyone is working in tandem to progress through a difficult time. Involving employees in the broader goals that apply to the entire company gives them a better understanding of what is expected of them.

All performance starts with clear goals and expectations. Employees have to know what their objectives are, and they need a tool by which to measure their progress and accomplishments. A Virginia-based PR company did just that, with great success. Using a consultant, the president organized a goal-setting session for every member of his staff during which they learned how to set and achieve their own goals. The result was an almost instant increase in morale, and all employees gained a greater sense of responsibility and importance.

Teva Neuroscience Has a Clear Focus

At the pharmaceutical company's Montreal office, goals are concentrated in three distinct areas:

1. Clarity of structure: Where do I fit in this company?
2. Clarity of direction: Where am I going?
3. Clarity of measurement: How do I know I did a good job?

Employees at Teva Neuroscience find value in the company's approach because it provides a true representation of their performance and goals. It's a simple process, but direct and, most importantly, it involves employees and helps them have a better perspective on their roles and what is expected of them.

Guidelines for Effective Goal Setting

Here are some helpful guidelines for creating attainable goals:

- **Focus on goals that most closely align to your organization's mission.** You might be tempted to take on goals that are challenging, interesting, and fun to accomplish, just make sure they are not too far removed from your organization's mission.

- **Pick the goals with the greatest relevance.** Certain goals take you farther down the road towards attaining your vision than do other goals. You have only so many hours in your workday, so it clearly makes sense to concentrate your efforts on a few goals that have the biggest payoff—rather than a boatload of goals with relatively small payoff.

- **The best goals are few in number and specific in focus.** Ask yourself, "What one or two things could have the greatest impact on our success?" Most people can only focus on one thing at a time, and to have a broad number of vague, constantly changing goals makes it more difficult for employees to clearly act on any one goal. Pick two to three goals to focus on. You can't do everything at once, and you can't expect your employees to either. A few goals are the most you should attempt to conquer at any one time. Picking too many goals dilutes the efforts of you and your staff and can result in a complete breakdown in the process.

- **Goals should be simply stated.** Avoid jargon and buzzwords and phrases that can have multiple meanings, or are prone to misinterpretation. Focus instead on using impactful, simple, and easy-to-understand language that is clear to all.

The Top Ten Planner

One effective technique for increasing alignment of goals between managers and employees is called the "Top Ten Planner." A manager asks an employee to take some time to make a list of his or her top job responsibilities, projects and priorities. It's okay if the employee only comes up with five or six items on their list. The manager does the same activity, taking time to focus on the employee's job, with the intention that both the manager and employee will get back together the next day and compare the two lists.

Once reconvened, the two lists are compared and discussed. Often the overlap between the two lists is only 40 percent or less. The employee learns what the manager thinks his or her top priorities should be, and likewise, the manager learns about an employee's current priorities. Sometimes, the priorities are never explicitly stated, and a manager might learn that a project he thought the employee had completed is still in the process of being implemented. Communication can be fickle and it is easy to get out of alignment on goals and expectations during fast-moving and dynamic times. The Top Ten Planner is a good vehicle to realign priorities and expectations.

- **Have "stretch" goals.** That is, goals that are not too difficult (which undermines one's motivation) but not too easy, either. It's the goals that are between those two extremes, perhaps with a 70 percent chance of success, that tend to be the most motivating. This is why its important to recast goals that had been previously set in better economic times—to provide employees a realistic chance of success.

- **Involve employees in the process.** The days of telling people what to do are over and the best managers involve employees in the goal-setting process to obtain their buy-in and commitment towards achieving those goals. Once employee commitment is obtained, their motivation, resourcefulness and creativity in reaching the goals skyrockets.

Periodically revisit the goals and update them as necessary. Business is anything but static, and periodically assessing your goals is important to making sure that they're still relevant to the vision you want to achieve. If so, great—carry on. If not, meet with your employees to revise the goals and the schedules for attaining them.

Once the "big picture" goals are clarified, it should be easier to prioritize areas of focus for employees and the organization's resources. Budget allocations and cuts should stem directly from these priorities. Making cuts to your budget,

---

Driving Goals from the Top at Turner Construction

Ken Jones, CEO, believes in connecting with employees to set goals for individuals and for the company. He hosts an annual meeting with a leadership team to analyze company goals, discuss what the competition is doing, and look at the company performance both past and future. The head of each department also gets the opportunity to present ideas based on predetermined common themes. The themes are also the company goals for the year and serve as a template for senior staff meetings.

The company has found that by including all employees—from managers down—implementing new processes and revised goals is much easier. At Turner, goals are based on employee input, rather than being solely created by top management and relayed to employees from the top. One very important thing that Jones has realized in this process is that employees know the ins and outs of their department better than he does. He values their experience and expertise to help set attainable and substantial goals, which in turn sparks a drive in employees to deliver and meet those goals.

while not completely eliminating your core service offerings, can be a challenge, to say the least. Knowing where your hard-and fast-goals lie can serve as an excellent starting point for determining where cuts can be made. If goals are set clearly and adequately, then it should be relatively easy to identify those positions and employees whose contributions are secondary to the company-wide goals.

Provide Frequent Feedback to Help Employees Stay on Track

Keeping employees focused on goals is best accomplished by providing feedback against the goals so that employees clearly know how they are doing. Use regular performance review meetings as a time to discuss corporate and individual goals with employees. Encourage employees to think outside of the box to find new and innovative ways to participate in the company's success. For example, managers can help employees establish goals that are linked to finding new cost-savings measures, or better ways of conducting an existing practice or procedure.

Traditionally, performance reviews occur once, maybe twice, a year. Consider for a moment the content of most performance reviews: a list of discussion items related to completed projects or tasks throughout the year. More frequent reviews of employees' performance and efforts to achieve set goals lets employees know where they stand before the work is completed. With proper guidance during the course of the year, many unintentional mistakes or behav-

---

Gucci Sets the Bar for Employee Performance

Robert Polet, CEO of Gucci, has helped develop a performance review process that is based on previously established behaviors he most values in employees. This has helped managers at Gucci better identify individuals who show leadership promise, and identify employees who can be handpicked for strategic tasks or roles when revisions to the business or mission become necessary.

As a result, Polet has found that during down times, it's much easier to quickly choose employees who are needed to step in to help work through a particular challenge, or serve on a special project group. The benefits are twofold: the employee is given an opportunity to further develop their skills and experience new levels of responsibility, while the company is assured of having the best people involved in a crucial task.

iors can be averted. Performance reviews should be given quarterly, rather than annually to ensure that managers and employees are on the same page regarding their goals and performance. More frequent review discussions should concentrate on goals—of the employee and of the organization—and should always include discussions about the future and development opportunities for employees.

Link Goals to Financial Rewards

Goals are far more likely to be met if there is a clear up front expectation as to what employees can expect if they are successful. Although intangible forms of recognition and rewards are important to employees, they also want and expect tangible monetary rewards when they have succeeded. This is especially true if you've had a salary or bonus freeze. Employees want to know when they will once again be eligible to receive raises and bonuses.

These days, companies have had to get creative in the structure of their financial rewards. If those rewards have been cut, they should also be reinstated as the organization can once again provide such incentives, especially for its top performers. Here are some considerations if you are still able to continue to award financial incentives:

- Place more emphasis on measurable goals that employees can control. For example, production levels, customer service surveys, or material deliverables such as product development.

Huron Consulting Uses Goal Setting to Motivate

Huron Consulting Group prides itself on employees who give 110 percent, so the process of setting and achieving goals is extremely important to their overall success. All 3,000 employees participate in a goal-setting meeting with their manager each year. Huron's CEO makes it very clear to all employees that not following through on their goals they set for themselves does not serve them well. At the end of the year, those who have achieved their goals are rewarded, and those who have failed to do so not only miss out on rewards, but they are also moved to the front of the line if and when layoffs become necessary.

The response from employees has been largely positive: because Huron offers a positive work environment, and generously rewards employees who perform well, all of the company's employees know that working hard will pay off in the long run.

- Identify stand-out employees that are most likely to leave or be lured away by a competitor. Create separate bonus pools for those employees and award them based on merit or performance.

- If stock options are under water, consider exchanging or re-pricing them.

Summary

Energizing a workforce to make change starts with a clear and compelling vision and direction for the organization. The organization's vision then needs to be broken down into individual goals for each employee.

Including employees in the goal-setting process is imperative. When changes are inevitable in a company, the planning process should be owned by everyone. For any degree of change to be successful, support is absolutely necessary. Make employees feel as though they have some control over their work when it comes to their jobs and their future with the company.

Revising goals and focus is a key part of surviving a recession. Business cannot be conducted as usual, changes must be made, and everyone must be a part of the process. In the next chapter we'll explore ways to communicate those changes and provide employees the information they need to move forward with revised goals and direction.

CHAPTER 2

Direct, Open & Honest Communication

- ✦ Involve Employees in Communication
- ✦ Two-Way Communication is Most Effective
- ✦ Techniques for Communicating
- ✦ Communicating Bad News
- ✦ When Layoffs Are Inevitable
- ✦ What to do After a Layoff
- ✦ Responsibility Must Be Shared
- ✦ Have a Plan to Deal with Rumors
- ✦ Don't Forget About Customers
- ✦ Summary

The need to know what is going on is pervasive throughout one's job. People want to know not just the necessary information to do the work they are assigned, but what others are doing and how the organization is doing as well. It is important to communicate to employees about the organization's mission and purpose, its products and services, strategies for success in the marketplace, and even what's going on with the competition. For example, I was intrigued to learn while working with FedEx Corporation that the most popular column in the company's internal employee newsletter was information about the latest developments at UPS and what that company was doing in the marketplace.

Common Mistake #7
Thinking your staff can't handle the truth.

Talking openly about a downturn in your business can help people feel they have some measure of control over the situation. What happened the last time business was slow? How did the company turn things around? What can be learned from that experience and applied to the present situation? Explore these questions in staff meetings or in smaller brainstorming sessions. Along with making people feel more included, you're also likely to get some helpful ideas.

In my research, the highest ranking variable that 95 percent of employees felt was most important was to be provided information they need to do a good job at work, which had a degree of significance that places it in a category of its own. These research findings correlate with recent research from Accountemps that found communication to be the leading variable that 48 percent of executives reported could best impact low morale in their organization.

One of the most common errors many organizations and managers make when times get tough is to not share adequate information with employees. In some instances, top management does not share information because they are uncertain themselves about the constantly changing economic landscape. In other instances, management tries to "protect" employees from fears regarding the potential of them losing their jobs or the ability of senior management to effectively handle the crisis. More often, these well-intended actions to protect employees backfire. Closed-door meetings and hushed hallway conversations create a sense of unease among employees and lead to speculation, heightened fear and worst-case-scenario rumors.

Employees want and need to know what is going on within an organization, even if the information is not always positive. There's nothing wrong with being honest with employees when a firm is struggling. Doing so will almost always lead to an increase in teamwork and dedication, especially if delivery of the bad news is also used as an opportunity to brainstorm and communicate with employees about ideas and plans for turning things around. Bringing employees into the loop during the downtimes can instill a greater sense of involvement and responsibility, which ultimately leads to increased feelings of value and trust.

Regardless of an organization's solution to surviving a recession, it is imperative that employees are kept abreast of management's goals and ensuing plans. Something as simple as a company-wide meeting during which the state of the organization is presented to all employees and financial or non-financial goals are clearly addressed can make a world of difference in easing employee tensions and fears.

Loss of Control Ignites Fear in Employees at Hearst

When the Hearst Corporation merged the *San Francisco Examiner* with the *San Francisco Chronicle* they informed all staff that there would be no layoffs. However, employees didn't believe it; the staff still worried about the stability of their jobs, regardless of the reassurance from Hearst that their positions were not at stake.

Duplicated positions meant, that one way or another, jobs would have to be eliminated. Employees left at *The Chronicle* couldn't figure out how Hearst was going to make the situation work. Furthermore, they had no idea how the decisions regarding who stayed and who left would be made. How would they be measured? Who would ultimately decide their fate? Management did not address these concerns which left employees in the dark and full of uncertainty.

Involve Employees in Communication

Think back to some of the national tragedies the U.S. has experienced in recent history, such as Hurricane Katrina or 9/11. After the immediate horror of each of those events, cities, states and the nation pulled together to offer support and assistance. It is our nature as human beings to want to help others during tough times, and economic recessions are no exception. Especially when we feel as though we're all equally affected, employees want to do their part to help their employer during tough times.

Managers and companies can learn from this behavior and tap into the good intentions and natural inclinations of its employees to help the entire organization. As cooperation and collaboration begins to take shape, employees will be ready and willing to participate in discussions, provide honest feedback, and even develop and present suggestions of their own. Opening up the forum to employees who would otherwise not be a part of such conversations can be enlightening. Many times, employees who are considered "junior" bring a fresh and unique perspective to solving a problem or developing a plan.

What to Communicate to Employees

Make sure to communicate and seek input from employees in all of the following areas of your business:

- Mission & Goals

- Financial Status

- Recent Changes and Plans

- Sales Prospects, Pipeline and Market Outlook

- Marketing Strategies, New Products & Services

- What the Competition is Doing

KB Homes Values the Input of All Employees

Joe Zimmerman, CEO of KB Homes, carves time out of his day to spend with his employees. He doesn't just take the time to be a physical presence, he actually listens to what his employees have to say. His open door policy applies even when his door isn't open. Every member of his organization is encouraged to drop in and share their ideas, no matter how premature they might be. When employees present concepts in the early stages of development, Zimmerman finds nuggets of value. He walks the hallways soliciting ideas and exchanging information. In his eyes, an idea coming from the rank and file does not diminish its potential for being a good idea.

El Dorado Furniture Seeks Employees' Advice

El Dorado Furniture in Florida held motivational seminars for all of their employees to discuss how the recession had impacted the business, and how they could all help by working toward a common goal of weathering the storm together.

Taking the time and making the extra effort paid off for El Dorado. As a result, employees reported a reduction in anxiety and an increased desire to do their part for the company. No matter what their role, employees came together to maintain a positive attitude, which was evident to customers as well.

Two-Way Communication is Most Effective

When discussing major issues like organizational changes, communication should come in the form of a dialogue, rather than a lecture, and questions should always be encouraged. Employees must be made to feel as though they have the freedom to express their fears and concerns, and receive honest and informative responses. Feedback sessions, departmental meetings or company-wide gatherings should ideally serve two purposes: First, to gather feedback, and second, to provide information.

Communication cannot be successful if it is approached in a piecemeal manner. Develop a communication plan that takes a longer term view of the activity. Thinking through possible challenges and developing systems to communicate effectively can better prepare management and employees when miscommunication does arise.

Allied Steel faced challenges communicating because all of their employees were being relocated to five different office buildings. President and co-founder Mike Lassner got together with employees and developed the following systems for accurately communicating information across the organization:

> *Common Mistake #8*
> **Keeping your company's contributions to yourself.**
>
> Many employees haven't a clue about how much their firms spend on their benefits, such as healthcare and dental insurance. Let employees know the specifics of your company's contributions. This becomes particularly important if out-of-pocket costs are rising for workers. Chances are your contribution costs are, too, and workers should know they're not alone in bearing the burden.

- Continually reinforce their message

- Frequently host events or meetings where employees from all offices are in attendance, creating a sense of community

- Develop newsletters with feature stories from each office

- Don't isolate great ideas to one office, which can promote competition rather than teamwork

- Prepare, plan and strategize

- Don't mistake daily casual conversations for effective communication, and instead have an agenda and schedule

- Remain flexible, open to change, and don't lose sight of the goal

Best Buy Suffers Consequences of Poor Communication

When Best Buy began experiencing financial strains, CEO Brian Dunn decided to take a look at the employee discount program. After careful consideration, a change was made that would save the company close to $15 million. A small change was centered on store brand products and wasn't well accepted by employees primarily because it was introduced out of the blue and caught everyone by surprise. Best Buy's social networking site became the primary forum for employees to vent their frustrations. Dunn set aside time to review the site and read the feedback from his employees, and eventually reversed his decision. Dunn's major error? Not discussing the idea with employees before making the change.

The company subsequently increased employee input by instigating online surveys to solicit ideas from its employees for cutting costs. Over 900 ideas were submitted in just the first three weeks, which led to significant cost savings.

Techniques for Communicating

It's impossible to "over communicate" with employees during turbu-
lent times. That's when the quality
and quantity of communications
should be greater than usual. One
reason is that more distortion occurs
in a rapidly changing environment.
The lines of communication that
worked well in the past may be inad-
equate now. Past communication channels may be overloaded, too formal, or
too slow to provide employees with information when they need it most.

> *Common Mistake #9*
> **Engaging in meeting mania.**
>
> In a recent survey, 27 percent of workers polled said meetings are their biggest time-waster at work. Re-evaluate all your gatherings, and think twice before scheduling that next Monday meeting.

Communicating with employees varies depending upon the situation.
Group settings require different interactions than one-on-one communication
does. The following are some suggestions for different communication formats:

Individuals

- Periodic "one on one" meetings with each employee
- Personal support & reassurances, especially for your most valued employees
- "Open door" accessibility to management
- 24-hour "news desk" on the company Intranet
- Message boards in the lunch room or the restrooms
- Chat sessions on the organization's Intranet
- Hotlines for employees questions and concerns

Groups

- "Town hall" informal sessions with management
- CEO breakfasts
- Brown bag lunch discussions
- Periodic "state of the union" updates on the business
- Department visits by top managers

Meetings

- Be open and honest in explaining the situation & challenges going forward, and take questions & provide answers

- Take questions in advance of the meeting or allow questions to be written on index cards and submitted anonymously
- Record staff meetings & distribute copies of these to those who couldn't attend the meeting.
- Capture employee concerns & unanswered questions for further follow-up by management
- Share information from management meetings with your staff

Some of the suggestions will work; some won't. By experimenting, an organization can discover what meets employees' needs best. In return for their efforts, survivors will respect and continue to serve the organization well.

Involve people early on. Managing is what you do with people, not what you do to them. To get the most from employees and obtain their commitment, start by focusing on them: who are they, what they want, and what they need. Then, build on that foundation by putting the best interests of employees first. Let them take part in decisions that affect their workloads and work environment. That can make them feel important and reassure them that they are truly making a contribution.

Social Networking in Action at MWH Engineering

Engineering firm MWH takes informal polls of its employees to determine which colleagues they rely upon most for help and support. In an effort to reveal communication gaps and strongholds, executives use this information to develop a roadmap of connections among employees. Understanding employees' communication connections has helped MWH develop a more solid and complete communication strategy and improve productivity. Known as a social network analysis, some organizations have adopted similar practices with much success. In addition to fostering collaboration the technique has helped companies such as Computer Sciences Corporation improve customer service and support and aided a lobbying group in pinpointing weaknesses in its networking.

MWH began using social network analysis to reduce costs by improving communication among their technology centers. For example, the center in Denver and the center in Pasadena each created programs that would track address changes among employees, yet neither location communicated the effort, resulting in a duplicate expenditure of time and resources.

Communicating Bad News

One of the most important things to remember is that employees are not looking for a sugar-coated delivery of information. The best way to explain the state of an organization is in a clear, concise and honest manner. If sales are declining at a rapid or steady pace, every member of the staff has to know. Sharing this information inspires all employees to take collective ownership of the organization's performance. From front-line staff to mid and upper level management, everyone shares a portion of the responsibility to an organization's revenue, performance and future.

> *Common Mistake #10*
> **Blaming those at the top.**
>
> If you're a middle manager who has to deliver bad news, you may be inclined to tell employees that you would have done things differently, but the choice wasn't yours. While this may temporarily take the heat off of you, it sends a message that you're out of sync with the company's leaders, which could be disconcerting to staff. Instead, present changes and the reasons behind them, including how they will help your firm persevere.

Including each employee in an honest, behind-the-scenes look at the fiscal landscape of an organization, sends the message that every single person is a critical member of the team. Feeling as though they are part of the solution gives employees the confidence they need to buckle down and do their part to pull the organization through a time of crisis.

When Layoffs are Inevitable

In response to tough economic times, more than 90 percent of companies have instituted some form of cutbacks. Most organizations prefer to reduce discretionary expenses, such as travel or expense accounts, than to lose employees and risk damaging the morale of their remaining employees. Nevertheless, quite a large percentage of firms have implemented layoffs, often in combination with salary and hiring freezes and, at times, reduced salaries.

Despite the consequences, sometimes layoffs are inevitable. Compassion is essential when broaching the tough subject of layoffs, both with employees who are being let go, and with those whose jobs were salvaged. For those who do not survive layoffs, how the news is delivered can make all the difference. In an effort to be mindful of potential security issues, some firms ask guards to escort the employee off the premises after their meeting with Human Resources. Employees left behind who witness this are left with an unpleasant view of the company and how they treat their employees. Companies who are cognizant of how employees perceive the treatment of those who are laid off make an extra effort to exhibit positive measures. For example, some companies provide free resume editing or writing services, job hunting assistance, while others might provide industry contacts and networking to employees who have been laid off.

> *Common Mistake #11*
> **Thinking short-term when making cuts.**
>
> If conditions eventually require you to let people go, wait until you can accurately assess the big picture, then conduct layoffs in a single phase. Making cuts as deep as you can the first time will minimize the loss of morale associated with staff continually waiting for the ax to fall.

If layoffs must occur, don't delay in announcing them once the plan is outlined. Waiting for too long leads to increased apprehension and may have an adverse affect on the plan for cutbacks. Further, when the announcement regarding layoffs is made, it is imperative to make employees aware of any definite plans for future layoffs or of the possibility that they could occur in the ensuing months.

While the bearer of bad news in most organizations is typically the CEO or president, this is not a stand-alone strategy. On one hand, a message of understanding and support from this level may proclaim "we're all in this together," but what employees need more than anything during times of turmoil is personal contact from those with whom they most frequently interact. One-on-one conversations between a manager and the employees they directly manage are one of the most effective means of communicating bad news and easing worries and concerns. While a direct message from a CEO or president is important, it should always be followed up by personal contact from an employee's immediate supervisor. A line of regular communication should, and usually does, already exist between managers and their staff. So what better way to provide reassurance and peace of mind? Such private conversations also allow the employee to ask questions they would not be comfortable presenting in a public forum, and this can lend itself to a much more candid conversation.

Discussions regarding layoffs should be had with all employees, not just those who are directly affected. Some companies hold an all-company meeting for all employees, followed by smaller group discussions with one's individual managers. Whether they occur in one sweeping motion, or in small groups, news of layoffs will spread quickly. Managers need to set aside time to discuss the layoffs with all employees, explaining the reasons behind the decision, the benefits to the organization, as well as plans for moving forward. In fact, in a survey conducted across a multitude of industries, over 90 percent of employees ranked "manager is available to answer questions and concerns" as either very important or extremely important.

Common Mistake #12
Making the wrong cuts.

If your company has had to reduce spending, be careful about slashing services to your clients. If customers are used to receiving certain benefits, taking them away can be a mistake. Likewise, be cautious about offering additional services, particularly if you plan to reduce them once the economy improves.

Reflexite Communicates Layoffs Effectively

Reflexite,the Avon, CO-based manufacturer of safety products, laid off more than half of a 75-person division in 2002 after the loss of a large customer. A sharp downturn in the economy slowed the search for a replacement client, causing even more worries for the president and CEO. The day the layoffs took place, he gathered the remaining employees and explained why the layoffs occurred, reassured them that was the end, and outlined his anticipated outcome. Going into even further detail, individual managers told remaining employees what pay and benefits those who were laid off received.

The result of Reflexite's strategy was that remaining employees felt more involved in discussions, layoffs did not come as a surprise, and everyone was on board with the future plans and goals. Since then, the division has returned to nearly-full operating mode and all but one of the laid-off employees returned when jobs once again opened up.

What to Do After a Layoff

Once layoffs have been made, it's important that managers understand that "work as usual" will not return immediately. Pretending that the layoffs never happened will cause serious harm among the employees who were left behind and have an adverse effect on productivity, something no organization can afford to suffer during a recession. Shell-shocked survivors often feel guilty for not being handed a pink slip as some of their co-workers were. Layoffs lead to other problems as well. Drake International, a global HR firm, conducted a large survey in April 2009 and found that employee morale, motivation and productivity dropped precipitously following layoffs. Indeed, 40 percent of the "undownsized" reported becoming less motivated, and 41 percent viewed their employer with less respect.

Inspiring employees during a recession, especially after their friends and co-workers were lost to layoffs, is no easy task. Many are still distracted by their own financial worries, and even if no future layoffs were promised, doubt surely exists in the minds of many. Working around these roadblocks to motivation is a chal-

---

Misconceptions of Downsizing

Here are some common myths about downsizing:

#1   Downsizing occurs quickly and centers around a definitive event.

#2   Survivors are glad to still have jobs.

#3   Time heals all wounds.

#4   The weak people are the ones who leave.

#5   Survivors who seem to be OK really are.

#6   People take what management tells them at face value.

The Realities of Downsizing

Here are some truisms about downsizing:

#1   When survivors are more involved in changes in the workplace, their reactions become less negative.

#2   The intensity of survivor's emotional reactions is proportionate to the speed of change.

#3   The longer an employee has been in a position, the greater his or her resistance to change.

#4   Though rewards and incentives may not lessen survivors' feelings of loss, they can motivate people and help them to positively change.

Source: Drake Beam Morin, New York

lenge shared by managers, CEOs, presidents and business owners across the country. This is the time for organizations to pull together and focus on the company's vision and goals.

Due to the severity of this current recession and its accompanying double-digit unemployment, a large number of workers are being negatively affected by something not seen for some time: cubicle graveyards. The average square foot per office employee actually rose in 2008 and 2009 after many years of previously falling, almost entirely due to the recession. According to Leslie Seppinni, a clinical psychologist, "Emotionally, workers look around the empty office, and it brings the depth of the economic crisis home for them in a personal way. They wonder: 'Am I next?' and a tremendous amount of anxiety and depression builds as they try to figure out what steps to take next."

BzzAgent Brokers Unused Office Space

Recognizing that empty cubicles were hurting the morale of its employees, BzzAgent, a community-relations firm in Boston, decided to offer empty cubicles to the self-employed, for free. BzzAgent was able to quickly fill the empty spaces resulting in increased morale for its employees and a nice place to work for those who took BzzAgent up on the offer.

One casualty of downsizing that is often ignored are the survivors. As downsizing analyst David Noer points out, "Survivors are left to fend for themselves, to somehow manage on their own."

Downsizing is a traumatic experience, not only for terminated employees, but also for those who remain. Joel Brockner, a professor of management at Columbia University and an expert in survivor guilt says, "When people react negatively to change such as downsizing, it shows up in reduced productivity and low morale. The real cause is that people's self-esteem is threatened."

Ironically, survivors are a critical factor in determining the future success of a downsized company. They are expected to assume additional workloads, work more efficiently, and adapt quickly to the new work environment in order to attain company goals. Managers must anticipate survivors' reactions to downsizing and help them grow in spite of the situation. Management must find ways to help survivors cope with their concerns about losing their jobs, their guilt about the termination of co-workers, and their resentment and burnout because of pressure to work harder.

Responsibility Must Be Shared

When employees are asked to take a pay cut or forgo annual or perform-ance based salary increases, it is important that senior management is a part of the same program. In fact, starting from the top is a good way to ensure that as the salary cuts or freezes trickle down, employees feel less resentment or frus-tration. Many CEOs opt to take the first and largest cut hoping to convey to employees that they have their best interest, and the best interest of the company, at the top of their minds. If employees perceive that their leaders are thinking beyond their own personal interests and making every effort to do what's right and best for the company as a whole, they are far more likely to assume the same attitude when the time comes.

JetBlue Executives Share the Burden

In an effort to weather a tough recession, JetBlue Airways CEO David Barger has instituted across the board cutbacks in every division and department. From halting orders on new aircraft to layoffs and furloughs, he looked at every possible avenue to reduce expenses. In 2008, he even went so far as to reduce his own annual income by almost $200,000. He did this not just as a means for reducing costs, but primarily as a way to make sure his employ-ees knew that everyone was sharing in the burden and to reassure them that they weren't in this alone.

Sysco Corp Starts at the Top

Sysco Corp. took a unique approach exhibiting sacrifice on the part of exec-utive management, and showing a conscious effort to restore morale and include employees in the decision making process. The top executives at Sysco volunteered to take a 5 percent pay cut with the remaining members of the executive team agreeing to a pay freeze for one year. The result? Sysco was able to give 50,000 employees a 3 percent pay raise. Not only that, the message sent to Sysco employees was that everyone was in this together, and that their contribution to the company was valued.

Have a Plan to Deal with Rumors

Human nature dictates that it's easier to believe negative statements of supposed fact than it is the positive. Because most rumors are clothed in a shroud of negativity, it's crucial to stop them at the source, if possible.

Withholding information is a great way to give birth to rumors that spread like wildfire. Merely talking to employees can ease uncertainty and let them know that you're there to provide information, not keep it from them. Gathering the departments together and giving each of them an opportunity to share brings the entire organization together as a whole. Most importantly, employees are receiving information based on fact, not fiction, and are better equipped to move forward and make well-informed decisions.

Marty Hauser, CEO of SummaCare Inc. in Akron, Ohio, has consistently made one question a staple of his staff meetings since he started in his position: "So, what's the rumor of the week?" He usually gets a few confused looks from the newer employees, but he has been able to smash plenty of rumors and clarify any misconceptions about recent company decisions or future plans.

"The reality is rumors are fun and exciting; facts and truth are boring," Hauser says. "But nothing destroys an organization quicker than rumors." To combat the rumors that can spread like wildfire throughout an organization, Hauser works tirelessly with his staff to ensure information is accurately relayed down the corporate ladder.

"The best way to destroy rumors within an organization is to be totally transparent and honest and candid with the staff," he says. "As soon as we know something, as the senior management team, we expect it to be articulated down to the staff."

Another way Hauser ensures the company's message reaches every employee is the "management minute," a taped message that is recorded and e-mailed to the entire work force. If there is a change in company policy or a news item that can be condensed into a quick-hitting, one-minute recording, it can be sent out as a management minute. When each employee signs onto his or her computer in the morning, a message pops up informing all employees that they have a new message and that they should listen to it.

Don't Forget About Customers

While employees require frequent and effective communication, it's important not to forget about those who keep your business going: customers. One of the most important messages to convey is one of honesty and stability. Transparency is critical. Much like employees, customers have to feel as though they have all of the information. If they begin to sense something is being hidden from them, the chances of them leaving for a competitor increases drastically.

Understanding the customer's needs is more important than ever during tough times of a recession. Recognizing the individual needs of each customer is the first step in working with employees to develop effective communication with each customer in the hopes of building stronger relationships. Furthermore, maintaining a true sense of integrity across the company, with the full support of all employees, is crucial to customer retention and instilling in them confidence and reliability. Concerns regarding additional costs, or cutting back on existing expenses, should be put aside in the best interest of the customer. Savings can be realized in other areas, but sacrificing customer service and on-time delivery should never be an option if it can be helped. Encourage employees to put their personal interests on hold for a while and always keep the customers' best interest in the forefront of their minds.

Common Mistake #13
Shifting the focus from the front lines.

Customer service counts all the more when times are tough. Are you doing everything possible to make sure those who are the first point of contact with your company send the right message? If these employees come across as indifferent or inexperienced, you could lose both prospective and existing customers.

Not only is it important to consider current practices and how well they serve your customers, gathered data from surveys is also an excellent measurement of needed changes. Often times, customer expectations differ from what a company may feel their customers want and need. Gauge your strategy by listening to your customers, and do so on a regular basis. The valuable information and feedback they provide is an ideal tool to use when setting internal and external goals or benchmarks. Then aim to surpass them. Giving customers exactly what they want is a great start, but going above and beyond their expectations will almost certainly guarantee a long-term relationship and increased loyalty.

> ### Regularly Obtain Feedback from Customers
>
> Customer surveys are one of the most effective tools you can use to pin-point exactly what your customers want and need. Use the survey results to determine the future course of action the company will take in customer service, product development and overall relationship management.

Summary

Effective communication is one of the most important activities a manager can do to help motivate employees, especially in difficult times. The best communication is two-way, involving employees in an active manner.

Keeping information from employees is never a good strategy; they are capable of handling the facts, as long as they are presented in an honest and to-the-point manner. Communicate bad news to employees as soon as possible in an open and direct forum. It's also important to remember the positive: even when it seems as though there's nothing to report but bad news, find the silver lining somewhere. Letting employees know the whole picture, but providing a positive outlook for the future, helps them feel as though they are part of the plan to move forward.

Schedule regular "state of the company" meetings, where an overall picture of the company's financial situation and progress towards goals are presented. Seeing the "big picture" allows employees to understand how their role contributes to the larger goals of the organization. Allow employees to ask questions in this public forum and if the answers aren't readily known, make a commitment to subsequently get answers to those questions back to all employees.

Remember, employees need communication from all levels. While hearing it straight from the top is good, they need the support and contact with direct supervisors and managers. Treating employees like individuals who are part of the bigger picture by communicating honestly and openly will lead to commitment, dedication and hard work on their part, an invaluable set of traits, especially during a recession.

CHAPTER 3

Involve Employees & Encourage Initiative

- ❖ **What Things Employees Can Focus on**
- ❖ **Top Ways Employees Can Take Initiative**
- ❖ **Ask Employees for Their Input and Ideas**
- ❖ **Involve Employees in Decision Making**
- ❖ **Questions Every Manager Should Ask**
- ❖ **Encourage Employees to Work in Teams**
- ❖ **Summary**

Communicating better with employees is the first step in empowering them to act in the best interests of the organization. But that's just the beginning. Once employees are armed with more frequent and relevant information, they'll be more likely to act on that information in ways that can best help the organization. The act of honest and open communication shows both trust and respect that management has for its employees. Adding an explicit request and encouragement for employees to get involved in helping the company can lead to profound results.

According to a survey I conducted of employees in a variety of industries, 92 percent of employees feel it is important for their managers to ask for their opinion and ideas at work, and 89 percent feel it is important for their managers to involve them when making decisions at work. This chapter explores ways in which each of these activities can be better done.

What Things Employees Can Focus On

Although it will vary from organization to organization, here are some typical areas of employee focus that can yield benefits to the organization:

- **Revenue Generating Ideas**—How can the company generate additional income? Whether it's new fees, cross-selling, or upselling, what new ideas could be tried?

- **Cost Saving Suggestions**—How can costs be trimmed, delayed or eliminated? What are critical vs optional expenses that could at least temporarily be cut?

- **Process Improvements**—What steps in the organization's processes can be streamlined, saving time, resources and money along the way?

- **Customer Needs & Requests**—How can employees help others in the company that are focused on customer needs and requests? How can customer needs be further explored?

- **New Products or Services**—What ideas exist for new products or services? How could those ideas be better developed and implemented?

- **Morale & Teambuilding**—Who would be interested in helping to improve employee teamwork and morale? What are ways this could be done at little cost?

As company belts are tightened across the country, managers and workers are entering into a new kind of partnership in the workplace. Today's managers have to create an environment that encourages employees to contribute their best ideas, work their hardest, seek out new opportunities, and overcome problems and obstacles. Workers are discovering that if they expect to survive the constant waves of change sweeping across businesses and hold onto their job, they have to join together with other employees to contribute more to their organizations in ways that they have never had to do before.

Employee Suggestions Have Positive Results at Champion

1. Consolidating mailings and shipments and recycling office supplies as often as possible led to a 20 percent cost savings on postage and supplies

2. Limiting and reducing the number of web conferences led to a 70 percent reduction in associated costs

3. Developing a strategy for successfully collecting past due accounts led to $1 million dollars in receivables savings

4. Selecting specific employees responsible for a closer review of expense reports to identify accidental errors led to $12,000 in errors being caught

---

Top Ways Employees Can Take Initiative

In today's fast-moving, constantly-changing business environment the need for employees to take initiative and do what needs to be done without waiting to be told is greater than ever. In addition to helping the organization save money, improve processes or delight customers, taking initiative makes the employee's job more exciting as they make things happen and get a reputation for doing so. Here are top ways that managers can encourage employees to take initiative and make a difference at work.

1. **Think how things could be improved.** It's the person who does a job that knows best how it can be done better. Encourage employees to ask silly questions such as, "Why do we do it this way?" For example, a secretary at Johnsonville foods asked why the company didn't sell directly to customers and was soon put in charge of what became a multi-million dollar direct-sales division.

2. **Think like a customer.** Have employees look at the business from the customers' perspective, asking what would make it easier to do business with your company. An employee at Kacey's Fine Furniture in Denver suggested changing the store's operating hours to times that were more convenient for working customers and sales instantly rose 15 percent.

3. **Track your own performance.** Encourage employees to track activity in their own jobs to build a case for improvements that could be made. An assembler for United Electric Controls tracked his numbers and was able to devise a simpler way to inventory parts that saved the company much money.

Common Mistake #14
Not asking for employees' help in expanding business relationships.

Ask your employees to think about things they could do to help achieve business goals without sacrificing productivity. You may be pleased to discover how resourceful they are. When appropriate, involve staff members in generating new business. This can mean expanding relationships with existing clients as well as identifying and pursuing new prospects.

---

4. **Take action on your ideas.** Having ideas is good, but let employees know that they can't just plop them on the table and expect others to run with them. They need to be an advocate for their ideas. An employee at Starbuck's pushed a frosty new coffee drink she believed in and with time the Frappuccino became a $100 million product for the company.

5. **Do your homework.** Show employees how to think through their ideas, what steps need to be taken, what the costs and benefits are, and how to collect supporting data. A part-time employee of the State of Massachusetts independently researched the state's Medicaid rules on her own time and was able to uncover an accounting glitch that enabled the state to obtain higher reimbursements. She received a cash award and special thanks from the governor.

6. **Build consensus.** Suggest that employees start with those who will most likely be interested in your idea to get them involved in supporting it. In the early days of the internet, an IBM employee sent an internal memo out to employees urging them to "get connected," along with action items they could take. He immediately got support for his initiative from others around the vision he saw for the future. He later was named Chief Technology Officer.

7. **Speak up at meetings.** We've all been in meetings that have gotten sidetracked or bogged down. Encourage others to play an active role in meetings, for example being the person who speaks up to say, "It may just be me, but have we been over this ground before? Perhaps we should summarize the choices and take a group vote for how we want to proceed." Others in the group will appreciate your intervention and you will help move the group closer to its goals.

8. **Volunteer for new assignments.** Whether it is a pressing problem, a special task force, or someone else in the department that needs help, encourage employees to be the person to step forward to help out. A new employee at The Gap in Toronto who noticed the company's policy manual didn't cover half the issues that came up in the store drafted a concise training manual that is now used through the country.

9. **Manage your manager.** Explain to employees how they need to understand their manager's priorities and fit their ideas into those. Encourage them to tell you what they need in order to do the best job possible. An employee at CP Corporation in San Jose told her manager that she wanted to meet once a month to review her work and get feedback about her progress. These short meetings kept her manager informed of her needs and successes—and reenergized her.

10. **Stick with your ideas; persevere.** It's very infrequently that ideas are met with open arms. Encourage employees to stay the course with those ideas they most believe in that will help the business. When management nixed one employee's idea for a flextime work schedule, she simply waited until a new manager came on board to propose the idea again, which was then accepted.

Shell Empowers Employees to Motivate

Shell Refining sought the advice of their "pride builders," otherwise known as their top supervisors, on how to improve the performance of one of its plants in Texas. Believing that these individuals were the most in tune with the other employees, the company turned to them to learn how to best motivate employees and instill in them the drive to help improve plant operations. The result of Shell's program was a vast improvement in overall morale, a better idea of what it takes to develop more top supervisors, and a 30 percent reduction in avoidable maintenance.

Visual Marketing Gets Buy-in from Employees

Visual Marketing, based in Chicago, Illinois, which makes decals for various commercial purposes, decided to focus just on the basics when it came to revising their goals. The company shifted their focus to innovation with increased employee involvement and empowerment. So, rather than focusing solely on output, employees were the ones considered to make the difference, and because of this, each employee went through teamwork training and was regularly surveyed for suggestions on process improvements. The company also revised its mission statement, and then had each employee sign it. Doing so signified an understanding of and commitment to the company's goals, which served to increase employee focus and motivation.

Ask Employees for Their Input and Ideas

Although I've yet to see an organization that didn't have an "open door" policy in which employees were encouraged to speak to their manager about any concerns, ideas or suggestions they had, in practice this policy doesn't work very well. The average American worker makes 1.1 suggestions per year where they work today—one of the lowest of any industrialized nation. Contrast that average with 167 per employee made each year by the average Japanese worker and you can see the potential that exists if only you can find a way to tap into that potential with every employee.

Common Mistake #15
Creating a 'no-ideas zone'.

If suggestions are dismissed without any real discussion, your employees will stop presenting them. Encourage staff to approach you with innovative concepts. If you can't implement them, explain why and let them know you value their input. Also, be sure to solicit suggestions from people at all levels within the organization. Often, the best ideas come from those on the front lines.

I'm convinced that every employee has at least one $50,000 idea if you can find a way to get it out. Consider companies such as AT&T Universal Card Services in Jacksonville, FL, where they get approximately 1200 ideas per month from employees, month after month, or Valeo, a French automaker that in a recent year received 250,000 ideas for improvement from employees.

Boardroom Inc., a newsletter and book publisher expects every employee—from receptionist to chairman—to submit at least two ideas each week for improvements Initially established to encourage cost-savings, the Boardroom Inc. program is called "I Power" and they credit the suggestion program with a five-fold increase in their revenues as well as untold benefit to the morale, energy and retention of their employees. Each employee is asked to turn in two suggestions every week, which are evaluated the same week by an employee volunteer. For many of the suggestions, the evaluator says "What a great idea!" and then returns the idea to the person who suggested it with the implicit permission to proceed to implement the idea.

As Martin Edelston, chairman and CEO of Boardroom says, "Sometimes the best idea can come from the newest, least experienced person on your staff." Like the hourly paid shipping clerk who suggested that the company consider trimming the paper size of one of its books in order to get under the 4-pound rate and save some postage. The company made the change and did indeed save some postage: a half a million dollars the first year and several years since. Explains Marty: "I had been working in mail-order for over 20 years and never realized there was a four-pound shipping rate. But the person who was doing the job knew it, as do most employees know how their jobs can be improved."

> ### *Common Mistake #16*
> **Crushing critical thinking.**
>
> No one wants to make waves when the boat's already sailing rough waters. But the tough questions need to be asked, particularly in a challenging economic climate. Reward those who bring up concerns and provide workable solutions, and be sure to voice your opinions with your own manager as well.

The first year of the program, suggestions were limited to one's own job until employees got the idea that the intention was less to complain about things than it was to try to think how you could improve things. The company even now has group meetings just to brainstorm and share ideas about specific issues or functions in the company.

The benefits of the suggestions are not limited to only saving money. Says Antoinette Baugh, director of personnel, "People love working here because they know they can be a part of a system where they can make a contribution." Adds Lisa Castonguay, renewals and billing manager: "My first couple of weeks I was kind of taken aback because everyone was smiling and everyone was open."

She recalls her first day of work in which she was pulled into a group meeting and within 30 minutes of walking in the front door was asked, "What do you think we should do about this problem?" Lisa almost fell on the floor. Why? Because she had just come from a company where she had worked for eight years and no one had ever asked her opinion about anything. Once she got over the initial shock, it felt pretty good to have her opinions and ideas sought after and valued by those she worked with. As a result, it was easy for her to want to think of additional ways to help the company.

The impact is both positive and contagious. "People became agents of their own change," says Marty. "There's so much inside of all of us and we don't even know it's there until someone asks about it. And in the process it just builds and builds." Adds Brian Kurtz, vice president of marketing: "It's a constant flow of communication. People are not sitting in a cubicle, totally insulated from one another." Here's some insights that we can all apply from Boardroom, Inc.:

1. **Encouraging initiative starts with taking initiative.** Everyone has an idea that can improve his or her job, department or even the overall company. Find a way to get those ideas out! Do something different, experiment and learn along the way.

I-Power Ideas

Martin Edelston's book *I-Power* offers a system that facilitates a process for collecting suggestions:

1. Prepare a short suggestion form and have it readily available at every meeting and at key locations throughout the organization.

2. Put a receptacle on the table into which people can drop ideas they have during meetings.

3. Once a week, retrieve the forms and affix them to sheets of three-hole-punched paper. Put all ideas submitted by an individual together. Place the pages in a three-ring binder.

4. Review all the ideas, comment, and ask for more information if necessary, at least once a week—without fail.

5. As soon as an idea is accepted, personally reward the person who made the suggestion.

6. Prepare a monthly staff report on suggestions received and progress made in implementing accepted suggestions.

2. **The system is more important than any single idea**. Set up a system that is simple, doable and fun. If the suggestion program becomes a boring burden, it isn't likely to continue for long.

3. **Stick with it**. The best idea may not always be the first one, but the process of valuing your employees' ideas will lead to more and better ones.

Involve Employees in Decision Making

Most decisions regarding reductions or changes come from the top down, but is that really the best direction? No one knows jobs or departments better than the people who live and breathe them every day—doesn't it make more sense to start there? If you're looking for a way to cut back on office supplies, talk to the person responsible for ordering them or managing inventory. If a reporting process is ineffective or costly, talk to the individual responsible for managing the process. A perfect example of this can be found in a reception-ist at Champion Solutions Group in Florida who received expense reports from field sales representatives via overnight delivery. When her suggestion that the reports be faxed instead of shipped was implemented, the company saw a 40 percent reduction in postage costs. This led to company leaders seeking the advice of employees for ways in which cost savings could be realized.

When employees believe they have a hand in a decision, company-wide buy in and participation is much easier to obtain. If the general consensus among staff is that decisions will be made with or without their input, the like-lihood of anyone providing open and honest feedback is quite small. Asking employees for their input shows respect and trust that you have in your staff and will likely increase the quality of the decisions being made. Ultimately, the responsibility remains with the manager for any decisions that are made, so col-lecting input from employees does not mean you are obligated to use what is shared in every instance.

For example, one way to involve employees in decision making is to let them assist with a downsizing. David Noer, a downsizing analyst, recommends that employees be involved in preliminary discussions so they can help shape the criteria on who will go and who will stay: "If you can involve people in the process and give them options such as job-sharing or part-time work-you'll be better off." Then, layoff survivors are less likely to experience feelings of guilt and depression.

Another way to involve employees in decision making is to have layoff survivors help management determine how they all can work together in the leaner organization. After downsizing, peoples' roles and responsibilities will be new, and they may seem overwhelming. Involving employees in crucial decisions will help secure their commitment. They will have a better understanding of what is expected of them, and they will see how their support and hard work fit into the overall picture.

Involving employees in decisions also builds trust, which is vital to sparking their motivation and enthusiasm to do their best. By working through issues as a team, management is telling survivors, "We're in this together." The way employees are treated during stressful times of change says a lot about how they're regarded by management. Are they pawns in a game? Or, are they individuals to be treated with respect? Involving employees in decisions will demonstrate that even when times are rough, management has their best interests—and those of the company—in mind. revising goals

Employees who offer solutions that result in cost savings should not go unrecognized. Incentives, such as bonuses, trips, or gift cards will not only reward the employee but inspire others to develop cost saving ideas of their own. Make the process fun and rewarding. Hold contests, departmental competitions or other organized events to increase employee involvement and interaction.

Implementing Employee Ideas at Intuit

The common perception is that it is senior management who serves as mentors for more junior employees. Scott Cook, founder of Intuit, lives by the notion that the newest and youngest employees are often the most valuable when it comes time to make changes and inject fresh ideas. He makes an effort to spend time with these new employees, and believes that he can learn from them. This approach, Cook has found, ignites the creative process and makes employees feel more valued.

This practice at Intuit has been so successful because Cook doesn't just solicit ideas from younger employees. For example, rather than take accepted proposals and assign them to more senior managers, Cook lets the employees who introduced the concept take the project and run with it. Not only does this put less visible employees at the head of very visible projects, it encourages innovative thinking and shows that the company truly values input from all employees, no matter their rank.

High Employee Involvement at The SCOOTER Store

At the Scooter Store, all employees are highly engaged in achieving the firm's goals on a daily basis. They do this through "huddles," the initial 10-15 minutes of a work group's morning meeting in which each employee-owner describes their #1 priority for the day and any barriers he or she has to achieving that priority. They all vote on the top priority and then their manager passes their collective #1 on to a second-level huddle that is held immediately following the first huddle. At the second huddle, the same process is repeated along with a review of the previous day's metrics. The manager groups can choose to resolve any or all of the barriers that arise and then they, too, vote on the #1 priority that is passed on to the executive team for that group's meeting, which is up next. On Fridays, The SCOOTER Store breaks its "meeting rhythm," as they call it, for "IQs," that is, "Ideas or Questions" that every employee has for achieving that quarter's overarching goals, which they refer to as "Rocks."

Questions Every Manager Should Ask Their Employees

Asking questions is a great management tool. Questions are seldom threatening if asked in an even tone, and they force the person listening to think instead of to react. Here are a few questions I believe every manager should routinely ask his or her employees:

"What would a good job look like?" Even under the best of circumstances, communication is fickle. Assumptions are made, information is misunderstood, and things change. This is one great question I've found for clarifying expectations and to more clearly focus on the desired goal and not the activities of one's job. By getting people to visualize what success would look like (in their job, in the team, for the organization), the gaps between the current state of affairs and the desired state become clearer and easier to act upon.

"How could we improve things around here?" Workers always know the best way to get the job done because they're the ones doing it—sometimes for years! Ask them their opinion. Donald Petersen, former president and CEO of Ford Motor Company once reported that when he started visiting Ford plants and meeting with employees, "one man said he'd been with Ford for twenty-five years and hated every minute of it—until he was asked for his

---

> *Common Mistake #17*
> **Sacrificing quality.**
>
> When people are busy, mistakes are more likely to occur. But don't let service levels slide because your staff is swamped. You'll create a standard that will be difficult to break once workloads return to normal. When a problem arises, take time to identify its source and correct it.

opinion. He said that question transformed his job." Other variations of this question include: "How do you think we should handle this problem?" "Would you like to be a part of this decision when it's made?"

"What excites you about your job right now?" Employees that work for Michael Levine, president of Levine Communications, a leading public relations firm based in Los Angeles, CA, tell me he routinely asks them this question. And if any of them reply "no," he immediately changes his plans to meet with that person about his or her job. Michael knows that when employees are no longer excited about their jobs, and are not learning or growing in their positions, it's only a matter of time before they will leave the company.

"How do you like being recognized when you do good work?" Dr. Robert Cooper, author of *The Other 90%* recommends trying to list five things that each of your employees value and then confirming that list with each employee. Great add-on questions include: "What skills would you like to learn in your current position?" "What opportunities would you like to be exposed to while in this organization?" and "Where do you want to be five years from now in your career?"

"What one thing can I do better for you?" A manager at the Mirage Hotel in Las Vegas, NV, asks her staff this question once a month. After listening to and acknowledging her employees' concerns and ideas, she tells them one thing they can do better for her that month. This simple question helps to build communication and rapport between her and her staff. Other variations on this question: "How can I better support you?" "Is there any additional information you need to do your job?" or "Do you have any questions I can help you with?"

The power of a good question can be immense. Use these questions to engage your employees, to improve the way they think about their work, and to get at some of the most important issues in their jobs.

Encourage Employees to Work in Teams

Rallying employees to promote an attitude of teamwork can make a tremendous impact. Teamwork, especially in troubled times, is critical. And it has to start at the top. When things are going well, it's easy for managers and employees to get caught up in the daily routine and not break out of their proverbial box. Yet, when times become more challenging, employees need to pull together to better address needs and challenges.

What does enhanced teamwork accomplish? It no longer becomes Company A's plan, it becomes everyone's plan. When employees play a part, even if it's a small role, they feel a sense of ownership, so when success is celebrated, it's their success too. Talk about a morale booster. Another side effect is an indirect way to dodge false rumors.

Establish task forces comprising employees whose objective is to identify better ways to work. Employees who have a reputation, and history, of being focused on the future or are exceptionally influential are ideal "team leaders" or good selections to serve as the head of a task force or project team. Remaining employees have the option of joining the task force or project team itself, or serving as the audience to provide feedback and ideas when concepts are presented. Avoid allowing work groups to become too isolated—doing so prohibits employees who are not directly involved from feeling any ownership. Furthermore, those employees tend to either resist or be ambivalent to any implementation because their involvement was not sought from the onset.

Once people know how things stand for themselves and the organization, their efforts need to be channeled into work that will make an immediate and significant difference in the company's focus and fortunes. This involvement goes far beyond the cursory invitation of "We need your ideas." Instead, employee involvement requires a level of rigor that shows the company is serious about doing things differently and tapping into the potential that every employee has to offer.

> *Common Mistake #18*
> **Tying your employees' hands.**
>
> Empower your team to make decisions that will ensure positive customer and client experiences. They'll be able to solve problems promptly, and you'll spend less time on customer service issues. Provide guidance on how to most successfully resolve dilemmas, and review staff decisions, letting them know what they did well and what could have been done better.

Whether at the group or individual level—or both—the organization needs to find new ways to do things differently, taking these ideas seriously and implementing them whenever practical. Efforts to encourage initiative should not be limited just to downtimes. It makes more sense to develop programs that fit the company's needs both during the recession and when the economy turns around.

Of course, it's one thing to set goals for employees to take initiative and it's another thing to really make it happen. One of the ways that management at 3M makes sure that employees are empowered is through the company's "action teams." Action teams are interdisciplinary groups of eight to ten people. When necessary, advisors are called in to assist on specific topics or issues. The team leader is not a boss, but a facilitator, an equal member of the team who helps to identify critical issues and resolve conflict.

Focus Groups Prove Beneficial at Texas Commerce Bank

Texas Commerce Bank held focus groups with employees to determine what procedures most frustrated employees and customers. Using the feedback, the company nearly doubled its $50 million cost-savings goal.

3M vice president Robert Hershock and corporate scientist David Braun formed an action team to figure out a way to dramatically compress development time for a new product. As a result of their experience they determined that a successful action team must possess the following three characteristics:

1. It must have a specific charter.

2. It must be highly focused.

3. It must be short-term and high-energy.

In addition, Hershock and Braun discovered additional key elements that they found contributed to team success to include:

- **Empower the team.** Give the team the authority to make decisions and then act on those decisions.

- **Let the team manage risk.** The group should be allowed to select the amount of risk that offers the highest likelihood of success.

- **Let the team control the budget.** Teams must make all decisions on project matters including financial ones.

- **Recognize the phases the team progresses through.** Some phases of a project are smoother than others. Be alert to signs that the team needs additionals management support or coaching at critical times in the project life cycle.

- **Let the team be involved in the reward process.** After all, who knows better what motivates the team than its members?

Guidelines for Fostering Teamwork

- **Identify key influencers**—Select key employees who have the knowledge, experience and respect of their peers to lead team initiatives.

- **Make it a conversation**—Ask leading questions, promote discussion and brainstorming. Don't rule out any possibility too soon.

- **Let teams do the problem solving**—Resist the temptation to tell the group what to do and how to proceed. Let them develop their own identity and process for proceeding.

- **Follow through**—Have recommendations include an implementation plan and means and timeline for follow up.

Summary

Once people know how things stand for themselves and the organization, their efforts need to be channeled into work that will make an immediate and significant difference in the company's focus and fortunes. This involvement goes far beyond the cursory invitation of, "We need your ideas." Instead, employee involvement requires a level of rigor that shows the company is serious about doing things differently and tapping into the potential that every employee has to offer. Whether at the group or individual level—or both—the organization needs to find new ways to do things differently, take these ideas seriously and implement them whenever practical. Efforts to encourage initiative should not be limited just to downtimes. It makes more sense to develop programs that fit the company's needs during a recession yet also can be continued and supplemented as the economy turns around.

The Five I's:
A Summary of Today's Top Motivators

Interesting Work: Everyone should have at least one part of their job be of high interest to them. As management theorist Federick Herzberg put it, "If you want someone to do a good job, give them a good job to do." Find out what tasks your employees most enjoy and use that information in future work assignments.

Information: More than ever, employees want to know how they are doing in their jobs and how the company is doing in its business. Open channels of communication to allow employees to be informed, ask questions, and share information.

Involvement: Involving employees in decision making, especially when the decisions affect them directly, is both respectful and practical. Those closest to the problem typically have the best insight as to what to do about it. As you involve others, you increase their commitment and ease them into the process of implementing new ideas and changes.

Independence: Most employees appreciate having the flexibility to do their jobs as they see fit. Giving people latitude increases the chance that they will also perform as you desire—and bring additional initiative, ideas, and energy to their jobs.

Increased Visibility: Everyone appreciates getting credit when it is due. Occasions to share the successes of employees with others are almost limitless. Giving your employees new opportunities to perform, learn, and grow as a form of recognition and thanks is highly motivating for most people.

CHAPTER 4

Increase Employee Autonomy, Flexibility & Support

- ❖ Reassigning Work and Workers
- ❖ Assigning New Tasks and Projects
- ❖ Delegating Effectively
- ❖ Allowing Flexible Work Schedules
- ❖ Making the Most of Virtual Technology
- ❖ Manager Accessibility and Support
- ❖ Ways to Support Your Employees
- ❖ Employee Assistance Programs Can Help
- ❖ Supporting Healthy Employees
- ❖ Summary

Once employees have been enlisted to get involved and make suggestions and improvements, they need to be encouraged to run with their ideas, take responsibility, and champion those ideas through to closure and completion. In my research on employee preferences at work, "autonomy and authority" and "flexibility of working hours" were marked as being important by 89 percent and 85 percent of employees, respectively. To the extent that managers and the organization are able to provide these motivators for employees, it can greatly impact their morale and performance in having them do their best work possible.

The vast majority of employees would prefer to determine how they best work. In other words, they prefer to be assigned a task and allowed the freedom to develop a work plan that suits them. No one likes to be micromanaged. Roles and responsibilities may be previously defined, but a job varies with the individual who occupies the position. Here is where truly knowing your employees becomes important: understanding their strengths and weaknesses allows a manager to properly assign projects and tasks. Take it a step further by allowing employees to pick and choose the projects and responsibilities they can work on.

Reassigning Work and Workers

When layoffs occur, the work doesn't go away. Identifying experienced employees and allowing them the opportunity to assume different or additional roles shows trust, confidence and interest in your employees. Changes in the business necessitate changes in the roles and responsibilities of all employees. Reaching out to existing employees and giving them the first option to take on new tasks, needs and opportunities, benefits the company as well as the employees. Giving the "undownsized" a new job or task has its advantages: morale increases, productivity experiences a boost and anxiety among employees regarding job cuts is drastically reduced. Additionally, current employees already have an understanding of the company culture, know policies and procedures, and have established relationships, so can have a greater impact faster in achieving what needs to be done.

Employees view a company that makes the effort to reassign workers as one that truly values its employees, which is likely to have a positive impact on low morale or commitment—a critical component to turning an organization around. When employees are trusted with new roles and responsibilities their sense of commitment and ownership increases—as does the positive view of the company and those in charge.

Located in Lexington, KY VistaPrint has made a practice of reassigning employees even when business is good. Their primary goal is to help employees better understand the business as it is rapidly growing. When hiring slowed, but the need for more employees did not, the company focused on reassigning employees to roles that would directly benefit their bottom line. Recruiters, trained in sales, now work directly with potential customers. As a result, VistaPrint has been able to sustain their growth, increase revenue and expand their hold on the marketplace. The reassigned employees are able to help the company and grow professionally.

Reassigned Workers Prove More Reliable

Recently the state of Massachusetts experienced budget cuts that threatened its welfare-to-work program. Rather than lay off nearly 40 career counselors, the state reassigned them to call centers in need of additional clerks to help with the onslaught of unemployment claims being filed. They were all transferred at the same pay rate. The state benefitted because even though a month of training was required, the counselors were familiar with the system and had experience working with the unemployed. The job itself was stressful, but the existing employees were well versed in handling the pressures. Whereas five employees hired from the outside quit within a few months, the reassigned workers remained.

An Alternative to Hiring from the Outside

The Liberty Hotel in Boston, MA had only been open for a couple of years when it already had to lay off 5 percent of its employees. Starting with the housekeeping department, several cost-cutting measures were put into place and many jobs were eliminated. Yet, an outsourced contract with a cleaning crew, which cost the hotel $13,000 a month, was terminated, freeing up money that was used for salaries of reassigned employees who might have been out of a job otherwise.

Across town, the Langham Hotel Boston added a bar and restaurant which created five new positions. Rather than lay off employees from other departments experiencing cutbacks, they chose five existing employees to fill the new roles.

Assigning New Tasks and Projects

While putting the brakes on new projects is often a necessity during a recession, they should not be halted entirely. Instead, select only those projects that can benefit the company and serve the immediate needs. Some ideas to consider:

- Research how the competitive environment has changed

- Uncover which competitors are no longer on the scene

- Develop a way to measure changes in customer needs and/or expectations

- Analyze existing products and services to determine which are the most profitable and which are no longer benefitting the company

Seek employee input during the planning stages to help enhance their motivation and increase the chances that the projects will be successful and seen through to completion. When employees are empowered by their managers the tendency is to work harder, better and longer.

Delegating Effectively

One of the major roadblocks to increasing employee autonomy is an inability of many managers to delegate projects or tasks. Delegation not only eases the stress and workload of managers, it also imparts trust to employees and gives them an opportunity to expand the scope of their work and increase visibility. Here are some essential steps when delegating to employees:

- Thoroughly explain tasks or projects that are being delegated—make sure the employee understands the reasons for the project, how it relates to the bigger picture, and has all the information they need to get the job done properly. Focus on the outcomes rather than how to achieve them, leave those decisions to your employees.

- Trust that your employees are responsible. When trust and responsibility are granted, chances are performance will be enhanced.

- When delegating assignments, make sure the employee is given authority as well as responsibility—micromanaging after delegation is counterproductive. Communicate this authority to others with whom the employee will interact, which can reduce roadblocks or resistance they might face

- Make certain that the employee understands how their performance will be evaluated and exactly what is expected of them. Establish a commitment and agreement with your employees, confirmed in writing. Uphold your end and follow-through with employees if they do not.

- Act as a support system for employees and keep all lines of communication open. Make sure employees are comfortable approaching you with a problem and agree as to when you both will follow up on the assignment.

- Continue to assume responsibility for delegated tasks. It is up to you to manage the process and ensure that the employees are set up to succeed, not fail.

- When a delegated project or task is complete, give public credit and praise for a job well done. Doing so will make the employee feel good about their work and encourage him or her—as well as others—to step forward in the future.

Allowing Flexible
Work Schedules

One pragmatic strategy to consider in tight economic times is increased flexibility in employee work schedules. This is highly motivating to employees, the majority of whom from my research have indicated it was a top motivator to them. Depending upon the type of work, flexible work schedules can also increase the efficiency of getting the work done.

For example, I once managed a work group that experimented with having employees work from home on certain projects. Everyone logged their hours and were available as needed to discuss their work. Not counting the commute time that was saved, we found employees to be twice as productive in the work they accomplished. There was less socializing and fewer interruptions, so employees could better focus on the work at hand.

Many employees struggle with how to effectively maintain a work-life balance without compromising their success as employees, parents or spouses. Research has shown that allowing flexibility in work schedules serves as a stress reducer and creates a more well-rounded employee.

Companies can help employees achieve a better balance in their lives by implementing policies that promote a life outside of the workplace. There are many options for increasing flexibility, including alternative working hours (arrive or leave early or late), four-day work weeks in which longer hours are worked on fewer days, telecommuting, job sharing, time off to compensate for extra hours worked, or even just the ability to allow an employee to leave work early, when necessary. In my research I found that 86 percent of employees wish they had more time to spend with their families.

Flexibility shouldn't be limited to just the times when employees are struggling. Many companies have found that by giving employees the option of a flexible schedule, or telecommuting, morale and productivity both increase. For some, the attractions are a reduction in the amount of time spent each week in a car and saving money on gas or mileage. Others may find it beneficial to limit childcare expenses, or simply to have the opportunity to spend more time with their children. Whatever the motivation, employees appreciate the option of being able to have some control over their own schedules and, as a result, feel as though the company has their best interests in mind.

Why Flexible Schedules are Worth the Effort

Companies who have enacted policies of working from home, or flexible schedules, have reported the following results:

- 34 percent reduction in absenteeism

- 1/3 fewer sick days used

- Overall decrease in cholesterol and blood pressure among employees

- 93 percent of employees feel as though the company cares about the work they do

- 91 percent of employees care about the company, not just their jobs

Making the Most of Virtual Technology

Times have changed drastically over the past few decades, due in part to continuous technological advances. As such, the way in which business is conducted has changed as well. Operating on a global scale has become much easier, and more streamlined, thanks to new methods of communication that have aided in decision making, smoother operations and ease of expansion. Fortunately, this has also opened up new possibilities for how employees work.

Gone are the days of office communications being limited to fax and phone lines, or face-to-face meetings. These days, some businesses operate entirely on a virtual platform with employees scattered throughout the country or world. While not every company is able to operate this way, a large percentage of jobs can be done outside the typical working hours of 9 to 5 or outside of the office altogether. As a result, in recent years, many companies have experimented with flexible schedules or telecommuting options.

Sun Microsystems Saves Expenses Through Telecommuting

Sun Microsystems allows employees to telecommute when possible, and as their work permits it. Those employees who averaged 2.5 days at home each week saved $1700 a year in gas and vehicle wear-and-tear.

While it's tough for some managers or business owners to welcome the option of employees working remotely, it's important to remember that employees are adults and should be treated as though they are responsible. Most employees will perform better if they feel empowered and trusted. Consider some of these statistics:

- 86 percent of employees today report that they wish they had more time to spend with their families

- Nearly 30 percent of workers in the last 5 years have voluntarily made career changes that resulted in a salary reduction in an effort to lead a more balanced life

- Almost 50 percent of employees value the option of flexible or work from home hours

- 54 percent of employees appreciate the option to leave work early to tend to family or child issues

- A large percentage of workers would reduce hours or pay if it allowed them to have more time for personal interests or time to spend with family

- More than 60 percent of workers feel that their jobs are part of their identity, rather than simply a paycheck

For example, the core of Home Shopping Network's (HSN) operations are their call centers. At a time when the trend in call centers leans towards outsourcing, often overseas, HSN decided to try something different: so they sent their reps home. While competitors, and other companies, field complaints about the quality of their customer service experience with overseas call centers, HSN put a stop to some of their outsourced work in the Philippines and stepped up staffing efforts in the U.S.

HSN currently employees close to 1,500 part-time and full-time workers and of those, close to 900 are equipped to work from home. Whereas most call centers fail at their attempts to allow employees to work from home, HSN has seen a tremendous success on many levels. Many applicants placed working from home above a higher salary on their list of desirable traits in a new job which broadened HSNs network of potential employees quite drastically. Currently, the majority of HSN's reps are drawn from infrequently tapped markets such as retirees or the disabled who are given an opportunity to have a schedule that accommodates their needs.

HSN reports that employees working from home is more costly than some of the alternatives, however, that cost is more than made up for in HSN's improving attrition rates. Once at a whopping 120 percent a year, employee turnover is now down to around 35 percent. The popularity of their flexible scheduling has been a huge attraction for job candidates.

What has this done for customer satisfaction ratings? They've improved quite a bit. As has sales performance. The most difficult part of implementing a work-from-home program at any company is trusting that employees will keep up with their responsibilities and not become too isolated. HSN takes the following precautions which have aided in their success:

- Take the time to carefully screen potential new employees

- Develop a training program that can closely monitor their comfort level and determine their readiness to be independent

- Establish a "home base" where work-from-home employees can go to reconnect with their team and other co-workers

- Ensure regular, face-to-face meetings with supervisors

- Host frequent events on-site to maintain a connection to the corporate culture

- Encourage social networking between work-from-home employees to foster a sense of camaraderie and support

---

SCAN Health Plan Encourages Work From Home

SCAN Health Plan encourages employees to stay home and work by offering free high-speed internet access and free office furniture. The healthcare industry is continuing to expand, in spite of the current economic state, but companies in the industry are struggling to find ways to grow without spending more money. Allowing employees to work from home eliminates the need to find larger office buildings, and reduces the overhead of those offices already up and running. SCAN found a way around this by allowing employees to work from home, and making it comfortable and convenient for them to do so.

Manager Accessibility and Support

Once employees are encouraged to take more autonomy, independence and flexibility in their jobs, it's important for them to be supported in those roles. For example, in one survey conducted by Gallup, 66 percent of respondents say their managers have asked them to get involved in decision making, but only 14 percent feel they have been empowered to make those decisions. When things change within an organization as the result of a financial setback, employees are likely to feel a bit lost. Even with solid communication plans, there can still exist an air of uncertainty and worry. Managers can set an example by involving employees in the transition process, providing recommendations for working with the changes and provide adequate resources for problem solving.

Helping employees sustain necessary levels of motivation can start by working with them to identify potential barriers to their success. Don't simply assume that there are no obstacles, or that all of the obstacles are evident. Look

---

Common Mistake #19
Fostering 'fear factors'.

Make it safe for workers to ask for help with projects. Often, your most reliable staff members will be the most overloaded and least likely to speak up. You may not like having to step in to remedy the situation, but it's better than the alternative: missing a deadline or losing a good employee to burnout.

---

to employees for guidance and input and allow them to point out barriers to accomplishing a task, completing a project or merely going about their daily duties.

If managerial or other staff changes occur—new managers are put in place, project groups are reassigned, departments have been downsized, etc.—it is imperative that all employees feel supported. No matter how large the changes, employees will feel as though they've lost some sort of control over their situation and they need support from their manager to gain back control.

At Edward Jones, employees are given autonomy to explore new opportunities within the company which helps keep employees highly engaged Some employees are asked directly to lead or participate in new ventures ranging from moving around within the office in which they are based to traveling overseas to launch new departments, projects or offices. The philosophy behind this practice is centered on Edward Jones' culture which strives to develop initiative and drive in all employees.

The company encourages employees to seek out new opportunities and if the fit is right, employees are given the autonomy to forge ahead with the role or project. If the employee is lacking in a few key areas, they are provided the training necessary to effectively move into the desired role.

Common Mistake #20
**Reducing autonomy
and teamwork.**

When business indicators begin to weaken, some firms revert to a hierarchical management approach with hopes of increasing control and restoring profits. Cutting back on opportunities for staff to collaborate and make their own decisions can backfire, however, especially among Gen Y workers, who highly value autonomy and the ability to work with others.

A survey of Edward Jones employees conducted by *Fortune* revealed that 96 percent of employees considered the company a friendly place to work, and more than 89 percent felt that managers followed through on what they said or promised. The vast majority of employees cited their reason for holding the company in such high regard as a sense of being supported.

Ways to Support Your Employees

Here are some guidelines for building rapport with your employees:

- **Take Time with Employees**—It all comes back to communication, getting out and talking to employees, spending time with front-line staff, and making an effort to truly listen to employees can open your eyes to accomplishments that would otherwise go unnoticed. No matter how small, the roles and responsibilities of every employee are a critical factor in the overall success of an organization.

- **Show Understanding and Empathy**—It's important for all employees to feel that their managers are on their side, routing for their success and seeking to help them succeed in any way possible. When employees are faced with life changes, tragedies, or circumstances demanding more of their time than usual, it is important that they feel comfortable discussing these scenarios with their managers. If they are met with understanding and a willingness to help, they won't ever forget it.

- **Be Available for Questions from Employees**—Best, Best and Krieger—a large law firm in Southern California—promotes an open door policy where anyone who has questions or concerns regarding their personal or professional security is free to discuss their worries with the firm's managing partner. Employees are facing some very real fears, and ignoring these can only make them worse.

- **Support Employees When They Make Mistakes**—Especially important to sustain employee trust and respect is for their manager to support them when they make a mistake. It's easy to find fault and openly criticize an employee, perhaps even in front of their peers, but if you take that approach, what you lose in terms of an employee's self-esteem and willingness to act independently and use their best judgment, you may never get back again.

> **Common Mistake #21**
> **Not looking to outside sources.**
>
> Your employees may be worried about the state of their 401 (k)s/retirement savings plans or how to manage their finances. While your firm may not have all the answers, you can bring in others, (e.g. from your firm's savings plan provider) to dispense relevant information and advice.

> ### Encouraging Employees to Take Personal Time
>
> At one Silicon Valley employer, a horn blows at 5 pm on Friday signaling everyone to go home.
>
> Encourage employees to refrain from checking email on the weekends. One firm went so far as to enable an automatic note that pops up when employees access their email reminding them it's the weekend.
>
> Closely monitor vacation days and encourage employees to use them, especially if they haven't taken a day off in a while.

Employee Assistance Programs Can Help

It isn't always necessary to develop a hard and fast program for addressing the special needs or requests of employees, but it is important to have a policy of understanding and sensitivity. During these trying times it helps to offer programs to assist employees through difficult changes. For example, ComPsych provides employee assistance programs and offers seminars for companies that have endured layoffs. During the first half of the program, employees are given the opportunity to talk about how they reacted to the layoffs and express any concerns that they have regarding the future. Organizations that have offered these seminars have found that morale takes a positive turn after layoffs. Such programs are available to employees who might otherwise require counseling or additional help with personal problems.

At Primary Freight Services of Rancho Dominguez, CA, management instituted a series of workforce training sessions in which employees were taught how to manage stress, job burnout, disappointment and anger. The executives at Primary Freight Services started these sessions because of layoffs, forced reduction in work hours, forced reduction in pay, and elimination of Friday as a workday. Understanding that these changes were going to negatively impact morale, John Brown, the owner, asked his remaining employees to attend these training sessions, which the majority of them did. The result: 85 percent of employees reported a positive impact of the training, and sales at Primary Freight have already risen by 18 percent from the start of the downturn.

Even with an external program to handle the underlying issues, managers must approach employees who are going through a challenging time personally with concern and compassion. Most importantly, managers should take the time to listen to their employees because sometimes that's all they're looking for.

Addressing Survivor Guilt at CIGNA

CIGNA provides an Employee Assistance Program that, among other things, addresses the issue of "survivor guilt," i.e., when employees struggle with feelings of guilt because their friends and co-workers were laid off but they weren't. CIGNA'S program proved so successful that it is now offered by the organization to its clients as part of their healthcare benefit plans.

Moreover, CIGNA employees and their families have access to up to 5 counseling visits for the same number of issues, regardless of the nature. The result has been a reported decrease in feelings of despair and helplessness which has, in turn, helped alleviate stress and poor performance at work. The Employee Assistance Program also addresses other immediate financial concerns and seminars called "Healthy Eating on a Budget" which are hosted by a chef and teach individuals how to cook low-cost meals. The benefit to CIGNA has been an increase in performance levels of participating employees as well as a 5 percent reduction in medical costs.

Supporting Healthy Employees

Even in tough times, investing in employees pays off both in the short and long-term. It has an immediate impact on employee well-being and helps promote a more positive working atmosphere. In fact, continuing to fund employee benefits that demonstrate a strong commitment to employee well-being was just one of five factors that Quantum Workplace found differentiated highly engaged workforces from low engagement organizations in recent recessionary times. There also is a longer term impact on the health of the workforce and employees' abilities to cope with stress.

Maritz Inc., the world's largest incentive company headquartered just outside of St. Louis, MO, recently announced a wellness program for its employees called Healthy Frontiers in conjunction with their healthcare provider, Great-West Healthcare, based out of Denver, CO. With a target participation rate of 40 percent of eligible employees, the program offers a comprehensive

24 Hour Fitness Focuses on Employees' Personal Lives

Founder of 24 Hour Fitness, Mark Mastrov, believes in showing an interest in employees' personal lives and thus encourages managers to have conversations with their staff regarding their goals and how the company can help achieve them. He also wants them to talk about things outside of work: family, school, personal interests. Doing so shows employees that they're more than just a part of the company's workforce, they're individuals as well, and the company cares just as much about that.

The approach of 24 Hour Fitness has resulted in not just a successful global business, but one that can pride itself on happy, productive and dedicated employees. Motivation among the company's employees starts with a sense of knowing that managers genuinely care about them as individuals and want them to succeed. Moreover, employees feel that their contributions, no matter how small, do not get overlooked. Employees who are reminded that they are appreciated tend to show higher levels of productivity, motivation and desire to do what they can for the good of their employer.

smorgasbord (no pun intended) of information, support tools and activities via a web portal accessible by each participant. Each activity can earn participants points that become seamlessly integrated with Maritz's Exclusively Yours® points system to be reimbursed for upscale merchandise and experiences from their 2000-item catalog.

And what a selection of support tools there are! From blood screening (25 points) to a personalized health assessment (10 points), monthly informational seminars (1 point each), nutritional information (including interactive simulations for planning a lunch or eating out at a restaurant), a virtual trainer to help participants plan an exercise regime (including pinpointing muscle groups for development and an online demonstration of each exercise); to monthly challenges (5 points each) such as the "March into Fitness" daily exercise plan, targeting 400 minutes of exercise over the course of a month; the "Strive for 5!" challenge, focusing on eating at least five servings of fruits and vegetables daily; the "Chill Out" challenge, which focuses on practicing four healthy behaviors to better manage stress such as adequate sleep and taking time for personal relaxation; to the "Maintain, Don't Gain" challenge, aimed at small proactive steps to ward off weight gain—appropriately timed for the holidays!

The wellness program supports two major strategies for the organization: 1) wellness/prevention and 2) education/consumer awareness. "Although there is potential of a significant positive impact on our healthcare costs, our real goal is to motivate people to engage: To learn more about health risk factors that affect them and to make changes to their lifestyle that can improve the quality of their lives," says Sherry Ward, Vice President of Benefits for Maritz.

Participants can choose from a variety of six-week programs, each designed to help them adopt healthy habits. All information is confidential to participants who are able to easily track progress against goals they have set for themselves via a web portal, with the assistance of medical experts, online access to registered nurses 24/7, or a health coach as needed along the way. Any results from lab tests, for example, are sent directly to participating employees without access by the employer, helping to assure privacy and confidentiality for every participant.

With a significant increase in heart disease, one of the leading killers today, a 70 percent increase in diabetes in people 30-40 years old during the 1990s (which leads to a four times higher risk of heart attack), and an estimated 30 million individuals with undiagnosed Type 2 diabetes in the United States today, perhaps it's time for organizations to help their employees help themselves to take responsibility and control of their health. Incentivizing a wellness initiative in your company could do just that.

No matter what the size, every company has the ability to develop a mentally healthy workplace. Employees and employers alike benefit from an environment that attempts to alleviate stress and provide support for all workers. Implementing policies and procedures that promote the involvement, health and safety of all employees is the most important step, followed by fostering professional growth and a sound work-life balance.

Investing in Employees' Health Pays Off

Research shows that companies that invest in the health of their employees experience a lower turnover rate, a decrease in employees with chronic stress, higher job satisfaction among employees, and exceedingly low rates of attrition.

**Proven Ways to Support Employees
in Difficult Times**

- Include employees in the decision making process, especially as it relates to their roles and responsibilities

- Encourage employees to develop existing skills and provide ample opportunities for career development

- Identify employees who show the most promise as leaders and offer them the chance to participate in leadership training and development

- Establish policies that allow employees flexibility in their schedules, and let them work directly with their managers to develop a plan that benefits them as well as the company

- Develop company-wide healthy living programs that promote a healthy lifestyle such as fitness, nutrition, and mental well-being

Summary

Employees aren't looking for ways to spend time away from the office, or use company time tending to personal business. What they are looking for are ways to better integrate the demands of their personal lives with their roles at work. Technology has helped created a work environment where communication is more streamlined, companies are better integrated, and most work can be completed from virtually anywhere. Tapping into some of these resources and finding ways they best work within a company can do wonders for alleviating stress, which makes for much happier employees.

Down times financially lead to anxious or weary employees. Pressures are coming at them from all angles. All they're looking for is just a little bit of a break. If work becomes too much of a burden, performance will almost always begin to falter. Integrating some of the creative ideas reviewed in this chapter will help employees and managers alike find a better balance in their lives and, ultimately, become happier, more productive employees.

CHAPTER 5

Continued Focus on Career Growth & Development

- ❖ Take Stock in Your Employees
- ❖ Linking Needs with Employee Interests
- ❖ Don't Skimp on Training
- ❖ Cross-Training Can Expand Employee Utilization
- ❖ Mentorship Programs Offer Valuable Development Opportunities
- ❖ Developing Leaders
- ❖ Learning Opportunities Can be Personal Too
- ❖ Summary

On first glance it may not seem like employee learning and development should be a priority during tough times. After all, if things are tight, does the organization really have the money, resources and time to spend on helping employees learn and grow? Shouldn't employees instead be focused on keeping their jobs instead of developing new skills?

However, upon closer examination, a recessionary time provides an excellent opportunity for both the organization and its employees to take advantage of available growth opportunities. First, most employee development occurs on the job, with existing opportunities to take on new challenges and assignments and in the process learn new skills. Second, with the hiring freezes and layoffs experienced by most organizations during a recession, the need for employees to take on more work and new and different roles in the organization greatly expands.

Managers need to support their employees in the learning of new skills and allow them to participate in special assignments, problem-oriented initiatives and various other learning activities. They should develop learning goals with each employee for the year and even for specific projects, discussing learnings attained in the debriefing of any completed project. Periodically, managers should also hold career development discussions with each employee, perhaps as part of his or her annual performance review to discuss career options and potential career paths that are available to each employee.

Take Stock in Your Employees

To capitalize on opportunities in challenging times, managers must first take stock in their employees to determine who has the interest, capacity and ability to take on new responsibilities and assignments. If you haven't already done so, take time to meet with each employee to discuss their job interests and ambitions and create an "inventory of readiness" for your staff. Ask questions such as:

- Who has skills that aren't currently being utilized in the department?
- Who is interested in learning more about other areas of the business, its clients, processes, products or services?
- Who wants to get into a management position some day?
- What does everyone want to be doing five years from now?

With this initial baseline of information about your team you will be able to evaluate who might fit emerging needs Navigating through a recession is an ideal time to tap the hidden talents of all employees and expand traditional roles to help move the organization forward.

Linking Needs with Employee Interests

While development opportunities are traditional motivators to most employees, during crunch times such opportunities take on a new sense of urgency. A needed position is frozen or another position is terminated, how can that work best get completed? A new project emerges, who in the group is ready to help out? New leaders need to come forward in all levels of the organization: Who has the interest and ability to step up to the plate?

As organizational needs arise, ask, "Who can best benefit from that opportunity?" and approach that individual. American Express developed a teaching concept called "Label and Link" that they trained all managers to use. As a development opportunity arose, a manager would label the task as an opportunity and link it to something that was important to the employee being considered for the opportunity.

> *Common Mistake #22*
> **Assuming one size fits all.**
>
> Remember that not everyone responds to the same incentives. Meet regularly with employees to talk about their jobs and what motivates them. What would they like to be doing a year from now? Five years from now? How can you make their roles more satisfying today? Layout a plan for achieving these goals at your firm. Even if you can't make binding commitments at this point, you can show people there is a long-term vision for them within the organization.

For example, instead of dumping a work assignment on an already overloaded employee, a manager might say, "Gary, we are forming a new client task force to deal with a new market opportunity and I immediately thought of you for the team since I know from our past conversations how interested you are in working more directly with our clients. I also know that you've got a lot on your plate right now, so if you feel you are too busy to take this on I won't hold it against you—there will be other opportunities in the future. But if you are interested, let me know because I'll take whatever time is necessary to help you with the assignment. In fact, it might even take more of my time than if I just joined the task force myself, but I'm willing to make that investment in you because of what I've seen in your potential on our team. Let me know what you decide and thanks."

More often than not, Gary doesn't need to think it over further and immediately accepts the assignment. To some people this might seem like a trick of some sort, but it's the essence of employee motivation. You can tap into an energy that employees themselves didn't realize existed if the manager is sincere in his or her approach and truly does have the best interests of the employee at heart.

Another developmental approach is to give employees an opportunity to experience different roles. For example, networking company 3Com believes that allowing those who work behind the scenes—especially engineers—to get out and sell to or visit customers gives them a greater appreciation for the value of the work they do. Sales people especially are constantly on the front lines— they see how customers use products and hear firsthand what they need, what they think can be improved, and what simply isn't working. Those employees in technical roles often receive customer feedback second-or third-hand and rarely, if ever, have the opportunity to sit down with a customer directly. How beneficial for them to engage in a dialogue that will help them do their job better and not feel as though they are operating in the dark with piecemeal information? Furthermore, when positive customer feedback is passed along, it means much more when it is conveyed in person and in greater detail.

Luxury Retreats Trains Existing Employees to Fill Gaps

Luxury Retreats in Montreal has decided to take advantage of its existing employees to fill gaps in staffing, rather than endure the expense of hiring from the outside. Some employees have been reassigned, while others whose hours have been cut are paid their regular salary to help out in emergencies or to take classes further developing their skills.

Offering career and development training to existing employees greatly reduces the need for, and cost of, future hiring efforts. By reinforcing the employees you have on hand, and tapping into their skills and abilities, you are able to develop a workforce that is ready and able to step up to the plate when times get tough.

Don't Skimp On Training

The Container Store has been selected numerous times by *Fortune* magazine as one of the "100 Best Companies to Work For." They strongly believe that their employee training programs are one of the major factors in their high staff retention rate and overall success. During their first year of employment, new employees can expect to receive 185 hours of training, about 26 percent more than any other retailer in the industry. As a result, for more than two decades the Container Store has experienced growth at a level of almost 20 percent a year.

Common Mistake #23
Trimming training.

Be cautious about cutting staff development budgets, since enhancing your employees' skills can payoff both in the short and long term. Do, however, make sure that company-sponsored trainings are effective and cost-efficient. Ask vendors for references, and leverage web-based training or seminars. If employees attend a seminar or conference, have them share their new knowledge with the rest of the group.

Though the temptation is great, cutting back on employee training should be one of the last things to go. Bernie Marcus, The Home Depot founder, holds fast to the belief that training is the key to establishing initiative and drive among employees. In fact, he attributes the success of his company to the longstanding practice of continuous training and rewarding for results.

Employees are the most important asset a company can have, for without them, a business simply cannot succeed. Employees can make or break a

---

Philips Makes Smart Saving Choices in Training

Philips Electronics made reductions in their training programs, with one exception: a program called Inspire, reserved for carefully selected employees who show the greatest potential. Employees who are selected are placed in groups and assigned a business-related project. After reviewing the way in which the program was implemented, the company decided to make some minor changes without cutting the number of participants or quality of the program. Rather than select extravagant locations for the training sessions to be held, they are now held in locations where the highest concentration of employees reside.

company, so developing their skills is extremely important. The strengths of employees can be the determining factor in how or if a company is able to remain a step ahead of the competition. One of the best ways to keep your workforce strong is through training.

According to a survey I conducted among employees working in industries across the nation, more than 90 percent of the respondents stated that manager support in learning new skills was important to them. Providing such support lets employees know that their development and career advancement is important to their managers and hence the organization as well.

One of the primary concerns management has regarding training are the travel expenses often associated with it. Over the last decade a large portion of training has been made available online or through other technological venues. In the two year period from 2001 to 2003, hours dedicated to technology-based training options leapt from 11.5 percent to 26.2 percent. Online options are becoming more and more popular, typically taking place as webinars or other online presentation venues.

To keep costs down, some companies have embraced the idea of in-house training led by senior management or top executives. All employees can benefit

---

Training on a Shoestring

- When training budgets are reduced, innovation is required. If space and dollars are limited, select top performers to participate in provided training. When times are tough, those with the most potential tend to shine even brighter and should be the first to be developed.

- Review existing training programs and evaluate which proved to be the most valuable and realized the most return on investment. Cut those which have the least amount of benefits.

- Take into consideration the effectiveness of current programs. Are they truly necessary and making the most of employees' time? Perhaps, rather than holding yet another sales program, find a more innovative topic that can help performance such as time management, organizational skills, networking, etc.

from learning from managers and executives in their own organizations. Programs can be a combination of general topics as well as topics that are company-specific using internal managers as trainers. Having internal managers as trainers taps into the wisdom of those more experienced both with the topics covered and the organization, its history, culture, and values.

Take the opportunity to make the most of your employees and develop their talents—hidden or otherwise—because it will pay off in the long run for skill development, employee engagement, and employee retention and competitiveness. Skills refined or learned in training are effective even when things turn around.

Southwest Airlines learned this lesson when they faced economic struggles after the events of September 11. With changes being made throughout the entire industry, the airline decided that all employees had to increase their ability to adapt to internal and external changes. So, rather than slash training, as was the norm in the industry at the time, Southwest increased the amount of employee training they conducted.

Playing Games at Southwest Airlines

One of the most significant changes to occur in the airline industry is the increased popularity of making reservations and conducting other business online. With customers not needing to spend time at a ticket counter, the majority of their experiences with airline employees extended further across the board. Added security, higher prices, new rules and regulations all added to the stress the average person already experiences with traveling. Executives at Southwest Airlines readily acknowledged this and put their heads together to find the best ways to work around it and make the customer experience the best it could possibly be.

Working directly with frontline supervisors, executives decided to help employees improve their adaptive thinking and better navigate change. Southwest employees were grouped into teams and "played" a Paradigm Learning game called Zodiak where their task was to create a hypothetical company. From there, each group was presented with real-life scenarios—some of which even occurred at Southwest—and asked to work together to resolve the challenge. Employees learned to tap into their previous experience and knowledge and how best to use each as a resource when surprises arise.

Employee Boot Camp at PCL Construction

PCL Construction ranked 28 on the 2009 "100 Best Companies to Work For" list for two very important reasons: their training program and their promote-from-within policy. The company has developed a "Pre-Con Boot Camp" that is designed to train employees on creating and maintaining strong customer relationships. The program is offered once a year to those employees who have a desire to move into the pre-construction services area.

PCL promotes a culture of employee ownership within the company and does so by focusing on promoting existing employees. In fact, in just one year close to 10 percent of employees were moved into higher-ranking positions. In an effort to make promoted employees successful in their new positions, PCL encourages mentoring by senior managers.

MITRE Narrows Down Development Focus

MITRE, ranked 66 on the 2009 "100 Best Companies to Work For" list, has taken a concentrated approach to their internship program. Known within the company as "shadowing," the program is open primarily to women who are interested in growing their career. Throughout the program, MITRE's female employees meet regularly with their shadow and participate in select meetings to which they otherwise would not have been invited.

Cross-Training Can Expand Employee Utilization

Cross-training employees combats boredom or complacency while benefitting the company. If staff size is slim, employees who are versed in multiple roles can help in times of layoffs or other reductions. Make the most of your employees; take time to explore their other interests within the company. For example, a member of the technology department could have had a former career in marketing or sales and vice versa, or an employee could simply have a strong interest in another part of the company. Utilize managers to provide or discover this information and use it to develop effective cross-training programs.

Charles Schwab assembled a group of employees from all departments within the organization and dubbed them the "Flex Force." When market activity was high, so was Schwab's call volume. This team of employees was on hand to field the additional calls and were provided adequate training to do so. Likewise, JW Marriott cross-trains administrative assistants to double as banquet servers when they are short staffed. In both cases, the companies have seen an increase in productivity and performance, as well as significant cost savings. In short, employees can easily be utilized in multiple ways for multiple purposes if they are provided the cross-training to do so. This strategy can be especially beneficial during a downturn to handle peak levels of work activity without adding staff.

Toyota Takes Cross Training to New Levels

During the recession of 2001-2003, Toyota shut down a plant for 10 months, but kept all employees and trained them. Toyota discovered that once it reopened, that plant had the highest global productivity and quality ratings of all its plants, which helped secure Toyota a higher market share.

Cross-training employees benefits the company as well as its employees, in good times and in bad. Toyota's unique approach of using a downturn to develop employees helped them establish procedures that aided even when things turned around. Not only that, employees found that they had acquired new skills that could help them in their current jobs, and that they could use in other roles as well.

USAA Discovers the Benefits of Cross-Training

USAA began a cross-training program for call center reps in 2007. Agents who previously specialized in and handled only financial inquiries were trained in insurance related matters enabling them to handle both sets of customers. Previously, transferring calls between agents increased the operating costs of their call centers and had a negative impact on productivity. But by cross training their reps, USAA greatly increased productivity and improved customer service by reducing wait times. What's more, when an economic crisis hit, along with Hurricane Ike, USAA was able to continue operating without increasing staff, something most of its competitors found unable to do.

Mentorship Programs Offer Valuable Development Opportunities

A mentorship program connects senior managers in the organization with lower level employees who don't report to those senior managers for informal development relationship. Providing mentorship programs allow employees who have significant career experience to pass on their learnings to other employees, helping develop them in the process. Employees with a desire to further develop their skills and career path are eager to learn from others in the organization and welcome mentorship opportunities.

Some companies offer internship programs for employees as well Especially in a large company, where options for a career path are numerous, allowing employees the ability to experience a behind-the-scenes look at a new role or department can help guide employees in their development. For a pre-determined period of time, allow employees who have expressed interest in moving to another role or division the opportunity to work alongside someone currently in the desired position or department. During this time period, transferred employees do not relinquish their existing jobs, and are assured of being able to return to their original roles when the internship is complete. Even if an opening does not exist, or the specific role is currently occupied, when vacancies do occur the employee who has completed an internship and acquired the necessary skills and knowledge is likely to emerge as a prime internal candidate. This saves the company time and money in conducting an external search to fill open positions.

Fostering Career Growth in Employees through Mentoring

SC Johnson has developed a Mentoring Steering Committee responsible for pairing mentors and mentees according to similarities in work experience, interest and skills. Over a period of 18 months, pairs contribute a total of 45 hours to the commitment.

All participants in the program, mentors and mentees alike, have reported a positive experience that left them with a sense of personal and professional growth.

Shadowing programs can be particularly effective in the development of unlikely relationships among employees. Companies that already have such programs in place have reported a relationship among shadows/shadowers that extends beyond the duration of the program. These connections, especially when spread across departments, do tremendous things for morale, communication and commitment to the company. Employees no longer feel isolated in their roles or departments and begin to develop a greater sense of belonging.

Young employees in particular are ideal candidates for shadowing or mentoring programs, especially if their current role does not match their education or desired career path. Many times, young employees or new graduates will pursue an opportunity with a company in the hopes of moving up or on to a job or department that better suits their background and interest. This approach has been particularly successful in companies or organizations that experience frequent shortages of adequately skilled candidates.

Developing Leaders

Continued training and education should not be limited to front-line employees. It has to include management as well. If managers are expected to lead employees through a time of crisis or increased demand for their time and skills, the employees must be adequately equipped with the tools to do so.

Some people are simply born to be leaders whereas others must be developed. Managerial skill sets vary among each person, but can range from a predisposition for optimism to possessing high levels of emotional intelligence. Regardless of whether a particular attribute is inherent or acquired, it requires development and reinforcement in order to remain intact. Many of the necessary qualities of an effective manager can be learned and even more can be brought to the surface or greatly enhanced during challenging times. The following are some characteristics that demonstrate an employee is ready to become a leader:

- Focus on learning and development
- Ability to inspire co-workers
- Empathy for others and a true understanding of their needs
- Dedication to employees' personal values and an ability to carry that through in their work
- Interest in engaging others and instilling teamwork
- Acceptance of responsibility for their work

Development of managers, or development of employees to become managers, is best achieved by combining personal and professional development. Each person should focus on key factors of their personal attributes as well as their career, including how they have contributed in previous positions, how they interact with individuals they encounter, what their values and beliefs are and what skills they need to acquire in order to get where they would like to be. The motivation to explore and expand on each of these factors has to start with the individual.

Stronger managers can help move a company from middle of the road to great, and can be even more beneficial when a sweeping recovery is needed. Investing in programs that provide leadership development is an effective strategy in the long and short term. If cuts to training budgets are necessary, concentrate on eliminating training for skills that can be attained through other means and concentrate specifically on leadership.

Estee Lauder Cuts Jobs Yet Continues Leadership Training

Even in the wake of cutting close to 2,000 jobs, Estee Lauder decided to salvage their leadership development programs. To ensure that this would be possible, they cut the number of attendees in half and reduced the duration of the training from three weeks to one. The theme of that year's program? Managing change in volatile markets.

Banner Cultivates a Culture of Learning for Leaders

The learning and development team at Banner Health works alongside the executive office to develop leadership programs. The result has been two effective programs that have produced hundreds of leaders:

1. **New Leader Experience.** Each month, this three-day seminar is held at the company's headquarters and introduces new managers to the company's overall goals. In addition, the managers are presented with resources on how to effectively guide employees.

2. **Leadership Symposiums.** These week-long development programs give leaders the chance to renew their skills and interact with other leaders in the organization.

Learning Opportunities Can Be Personal Too

Training shouldn't end at job-related tasks and knowledge. At a time when employees will become more interested in the financial health of the company, it is important for them to understand the information being presented. Making additional training available to all employees regarding financial matters will not only aid in their understanding of the company's financial situation, but will help encourage a commitment to help turn things around. If employees feel as though they are a part of the process by understanding how their jobs contribute to the overall performance of the company, they are far more likely to jump on board and work that much harder to contribute.

The best learning cultures promote learning of all types, not just job-specific training. Offering programs that speak to employee emotional and mental well-being is one way of showing you have employees' best interests at heart. For example, if company financial goals are being revised, chances are that employees' personal finances will be impacted as well. Providing access to information: webcasts, online seminars, etc., regarding financial management or investments is a great way to help employees plan for their future as well as be more open to changes within the company. Helping employees learn how to better manage their finances can help reduce stress levels at work, as well.

Here are some ways that companies are helping develop employees:

- **GSK Heads Off Stress at the Pass** GlaxoSmithKline offers a seminar focused on personal resilience to teach employees ways to prevent stress and succeed in their jobs. A group of employees is assigned the task of pointing out work-related pressures within their departments and present suggestions as to how they might be combated. The aim of the program is to address life pressures as well, with the belief that for employees to be successful they must be happy. Since its inception, GSKs stress management program has reduced work-related and stress induced illnesses in employees by nearly 60 percent—which also resulted in a 29 percent decrease in absenteeism for health issues.

- **Ernst & Young has offered stress management programs to employees for nearly 20 years.** Known as EY/Assist, the program has been responsible for the development of policies such as allowing employees to bring their children along on business trips and company-provided consultation services. Most recently, sponsors of the program developed a blog wherein employees can exchange tips for effective stress management. 76 percent of Ernst & Young employees reported stress levels at moderate to great before taking advantage of this stress management program. The same employees were surveyed again, after enrolling in the program, and 50 percent stated that they had seen a marked improvement in their stress levels with 62 percent feeling their productivity had improved.

- **MetLife Helps Revise Plans for the Future.** MetLife, one of the largest providers of employee benefits, offers retirement education seminars in various companies. The workshops are free and are presented by Certified Financial Planners offering advice and instruction on financing retirement, for employees of all ages. At the end of the seminar, close to half of the attendees chose to take advantage of the opportunity to meet with a retirement specialist. Assuming an active role in helping employees plan for the future shows a company's concern for all aspects of employees' lives. Frequently, seminars can include discussions that go beyond financing retirement to planning activities when work is no longer part of the daily routine. An opportunity for employees to ask questions that they might not get answered elsewhere can set the wheels in motion for better planning.

- **KPMG Offers a Variety of Training Seminars.** Tax and advisory firm, KPMG, offers training and educational programs to employees and, more recently, webinars on financial planning and surviving a down economy. They have also added two seminars on stress and weight management combined with personal coaches to help establish goals and stick to them. The cost to keep these programs operating is exceptionally low, especially considering the tremendous benefit to the employees and the company. Employees were extremely appreciate of the forward thinking exhibited by the company regarding their health and well-being and, as a result, productivity and positive attitudes increased drastically.

- **Fidelity Offers Options for Seminars.** Fidelity Investments offers financial web-based seminars that allow employees to participate from their office or home. Fidelity has found that of all attendees at its seminars, half make some kind of change to their retirement goals within a couple weeks. A focus on education, and making it simple for employees to revise their financial goals and plans, has made such seminars successful in the workplace.

Offering such programs to employees can aid them in sorting out worries that are most likely at the forefront of their minds: living expenses, healthcare, insurance, investments, and general retirement planning. A better understanding of their financial situation can help employees focus more on long-term plans for their career. These days, employees are no longer relying on their 401(k)s for retirement savings and are looking for alternate means to secure their financial future. Taking steps to ease such worries is beneficial to the company, and requires very little cost or effort.

Increasing Training to Increase Sales at Glass Doctor

The Glass Doctor in Florida encourages its sales people to make in-person calls on customers rather than sit on the phone all day. Most sales people are specialized in a certain type of glass: residential, auto or commercial. The company developed a program at its training facility to train its sales people on all of the products. Role-playing sessions designed to provide realistic sales scenarios also helped give the employees honest feedback on their approach and sales strategies.

The goal of the program was to position themselves in the marketplace as a comprehensive distributor in the glass industry, sharpen customer service and increase sales. The result was an added insight into untapped leads and a polished sales force that has helped the company increase sales and revenue.

Summary

Taking an action-oriented approach in helping employees to develop new skills and responsibilities can make for exciting and productive times for everyone, as well as to better meet the changing needs of the organization. In my research with employees, management support of employees who want to learn new skills was one of the top motivators reported by today's employees at over 90 percent. Since all development is essentially self development, providing opportunities to employees to learn and grow benefits both them and the organization.

Properly trained employees perform better at their jobs and tend to work harder. Whether in the form of preparation for a new or advanced role, or a program designed to promote growth within an existing role, all employees need continued education and development. Not only will this help when layoffs have reduced staff, but not workload, it provides a foundation of well-rounded employees who are willing and able to take on new tasks or projects when the need arises. Cuts to training programs and opportunities are sometimes inevitable, but avoid the temptation to eliminate them altogether or even put them on indefinite hold. Simply revising what is already in place, for example, by using more online training or company managers or trainers, can keep training opportunities alive and available to employees. Consider it a further investment in the value of employees, as development of leaders and motivated employees will serve a company well in good times and bad.

There is no better time than a downturn to invest in employees. Singling out the most promising employees and providing opportunities for them to further develop their skills and strengths can help in bad times as well as good. Money and time spent on training during a recession has a return that can last for years as the knowledge gained and the skills acquired stay with employees. Furthermore, cultivating a culture of development with employees can boost a company's reputation as one focused on providing employee development, clear career paths, and on-the-job training for employees to ensure their success and advancement.

Nursing Shortages Lead to Innovative Ideas

New graduate nurses often face culture shock when moving into a full-time role in a hospital environment. To ease this transition, some hospitals have made adjustments to their entry programs:

- Provide online evaluation systems to track progress
- Establish regular meetings with a mentor to discuss the evaluation
- Develop an easily accessible curriculum program
- Select individuals from various departments to conduct trainings so that newly hired employees establish relationships outside of those with whom they directly work
- Recruit volunteers, especially previous or retired employees, to serve as mentors if existing employees cannot afford to take the time

CHAPTER 6

Recognize & Reward High Performance

◆ **The Limitations of Cash as a Motivator**

◆ **A Simple "Thanks" Will Do**

◆ **Four Types of Praise**

◆ **Elements of a Good Praising**

◆ **Rewards Don't Have to be Expensive**

◆ **Peer-Initiated Recognition is Powerful**

◆ **Rewarding Employees as a Team**

◆ **Summary**

The most proven driver of desired behavior and performance known to mankind is the notion that "You get what you reward." As a manager in any organization you will get more of the desired behavior and performance you want from your employees by taking the time to notice, recognize and reward them when they excel in their work.

In my research I've found that it's almost universal (99+ percent) that today's employees want and expect to be recognized when they do good work, although only 12 percent report that they are consistently recognized in ways that are important to them and 85 percent of employees say they feel over worked and under-appreciated where they work today.

Driving performance of any kind is a function of its consequences, and positive consequences such as employee recognition are needed to systematically reinforce successes and desired behavior when those occur. Positive consequences bring about positive results and what you do doesn't have to cost a lot of money to be effective. When budgets don't allow for lavish celebrations, incentive trips or expensive rewards, this should not serve as an excuse for not recognizing employees. Quite the contrary. Employees will tend to be more responsive to intangible and interpersonal recognition with little, if any, financial cost.

During tough times the need for employees to feel valued greatly increases and timely, sincere, and specific forms of appreciation should be more frequently expressed for a job well done. Managers need to increase their focus on employee recognition, exploring more ways to get creative in showing employees that what they do matters. More than anything, employees need to feel valued in today's business climate.

Common Mistake #24
Eliminating incentives.

Cutting budgets shouldn't mean cutting rewards. Low-and no-cost incentives can make a significant positive impact. Be creative in how you recognize outstanding performance. Tickets to an art exhibit, an afternoon off, praise at a meeting or a personal thank-you note for going above and beyond are inexpensive ways to show appreciation.

When cash flows freely, many companies don't hold back on rewards, incentives and perks for employees. During the good times, such rewards are often an essential motivation and retention strategy. However, in the height of a recession with no certain end in sight, many companies have found that they can't afford to reward employees as they did before, but they also can't afford not to reward them as well. Research by Accountemps found that 19 percent of executives cited "recognition programs" as one of the best remedies for low employee morale, the second highest category. And, 13 percent of these executives reported that offering financial rewards was an important aspect for improving employee morale in tough times, followed closely by "unexpected rewards" that 11 percent of executives felt helped to improve morale.

> ### Common Mistake #25
> **Equating busy with productive.**
>
> Don't base employee recognition on who's logging the most hours or providing the most detailed project updates. Instead, reward people based on the results they generate against company objectives and the progress they make along the way.

According to a recent survey by incentive industry leader Maritz, employees who work at recognition-oriented companies are:

- 5 times more likely to feel valued

- 7 times more likely to stay with the company

- 6 times more likely to invest in the company

- 11 times more likely to feel completely committed

Additionally, a 2008 Tower Perrins study reports that committed employees deliver 57 percent more effort than uncommitted ones. Every company needs this commitment and effort from employees, especially in difficult times.

The Limitations of Cash as a Motivator

When it comes to rewards, most managers think money is the top motivator for their employees. Money is, of course, important, but today's employees value many other things. Surprisingly, some of the top motivators, such as praise, involvement, and support, have the least financial cost.

Cash has other limitations as well. In a 2008 study by Maritz, the following anomalies about cash rewards were revealed:

- Rewards that are strictly monetary are not as effective as non-cash based items. Because cash tends to be less personal, the opportunity to develop and grow interpersonal relationships is hindered with its use.

- Monetary rewards do little to establish a link between the behavior and the incentive. Instead of furthering company values, cash diminishes them and promotes a culture of unnecessary spending.

Cash rewards have one more problem. In most organizations, performance reviews—and corresponding salary increases—occur only once a year (even less if salaries are frozen), whereas the things that cause someone to be motivated today are typically forms of recognition in response to recently completed tasks such as, being thanked for doing a good job, being involved in decision making, being supported by one's manager, etc. To motivate employees, managers need to recognize and reward achievements and progress toward goals on a daily basis, and not wait to recognize employees at year end or at their annual review.

There is a common misconception about the use of rewards and recognition to motivate employees: that it costs a company too much money—money that should be devoted to other purposes, especially when budgets are tight. While this misconception is problem enough in times of high economic growth and prosperity, it is particularly damaging in down economic times. Rewards, recognition, and praise do not need to be lavish or expensive to be effective. Most motivating and meaningful forms of recognition, as reported by today's employees, typically cost little or nothing at all.

A Simple "Thanks" Will Do

It all starts with a thank you, and sometimes that's all it takes. Most employees don't just need to be thanked, they *expect* to be thanked for something they've done, and they expect that thanks to happen immediately or soon after when they have performed well. Waiting too long shows indifference and that it was really more of an afterthought or something you've put off. Even affirmation from co-workers is highly valued by most employees today.

In tough times, management should recognize and reward performance that makes a difference. Employees feel ambiguous and unclear in times of flux, and they are likely to be skeptical about their future with the company. So that vital employees don't jump ship, they need to feel that their hard work and devotion is appreciated. Now, more than ever, management must recognize them. Recognition can go a long way to keeping employees motivated, satisfied, and committed.

Managers should recognize employees for their progress toward an achievement of desired performance goals. They should show appreciation for small accomplishments as well as big ones. The recognition must be ongoing to reinforce employees' need to feel that they're doing a good job.

Employees need to feel as though their efforts are well spent, even if the results can realistically be classified as baby steps. Focusing on accomplishments gives your employees the encouragement they need to keep moving forward in a difficult time. If they feel as though they're consistently giving their all, only to hear it's not enough, the time will come when they'll give up or burn out.

> *Common Mistake #26*
> **Not appreciating your customer.**
>
> If you genuinely enjoy what you do—and those you do it for—it shows. Let your clients and customers know they're appreciated and respected at every opportunity.

Overcoming the cloud of negative energy that befalls an organization during the downtimes can be gradually chipped away by taking the time to point out your employees' strengths and what they have done well. Forget about shortcomings and mistakes for the immediate future and instead focus on the positive where possible. So many small successes go unnoticed because they are merely a part of a large accomplishment, leaving many key contributors in the shadow of those who ultimately receive the greatest praise and recognition.

Recognizing Positive Feedback From Others

Jeanette Pagliaro, co-owner of Visiting Angels, an elder-care service, often receives positive feedback from clients or supervisors about her employees. Employees who receive such pointed recognition are given "Angel Bucks," which can be used to buy prizes at an auction sponsored by the company.

Four Types of Praise

In my research I've found that simple praise represents four of the top ten categories of desired employee motivators when employees do good work. I identified four types of praise:

- **Personal Praise**—face to face thanks and acknowledgement for a job well done

- **Written Praise**—a written note or formal letter of thanks

- **Electronic Praise**—personal thanks and acknowledgement via e-mail or voicemail

- **Public Praise**—recognition in front of one or more people, in a public forum such as a meeting or celebration, or broad form of communication such as a newsletter or newspaper.

At first glance these different forms of praise might all seem like a single dimension (employee praise), but I've learned that this is not the case. Each of these dimensions is mutually exclusive and provides a different value and meaning to an employee than the other forms of praise. It means something different, for example, to be praised to one's face versus being sent an email or note or doing the praise before others.

At meetings, allocate some time for recognition of outstanding effort or the sharing of success stories. Sharing a public praise, such as reading a positive letter from a satisfied customer, can be an effective way to start a meeting. Some companies even open the floor to anyone to share good news, perhaps not moving on to the agenda until several items have been identified by the group.

Ending meetings on a high note, especially those whose agendas are laden with less-than-happy line items, is another great way to remind employees that even in downtimes there are still good things happening.

Elements of a Good Praising

In the workplace, praise is priceless, yet it costs nothing. In one recent poll, workers named a personal praising from their manager for doing a good job as the #1 most motivating incentive, yet almost 60 percent of employees say they seldom if ever receive such a praising from their manager. Although giving an effective praise may seem like common sense, a lot of people have never learned how to do it. I suggest an acronym "ASAP-cubed" to remember the essential elements of a good praising. That is, praise should be: as soon, as sincere, as specific, as personal, as positive, and as proactive, as possible.

- **As soon**—Timing is very important when using positive reinforcement according to extensive research on the topic. You need to give others praise as soon as the achievement is complete or the desired behavior is displayed. You might even interrupt someone who's in a meeting to provide a quick word of praise, until you are able to discuss the achievement with them at greater length.

- **As sincere**—Words alone can fall flat if you are not sincere in why you are praising. You need to praise because you are truly appreciative and excited about the other person's success, otherwise it may come across as a manipulative tactic—something you are doing only when you want an employee to work late, for example.

- **As specific**—Avoid generalities in favor of details of the achievement. "You really turned that angry customer around--you let him unload all his emotions and then focused on what you could do for him, not what you could not do for him." Specifics give credibility to your praising and also serve a practical purpose of stating exactly what was good about your behavior or achievement.

- **As personal**—A key to conveying your message is praising in person, face-to-face. This shows the activity is important enough to you to put aside everything else you have to do and just focus on the other person. Since we all have limited time, those things you do personally indicate they have a higher value to you.

- **As positive**—Too many managers undercut praise with a concluding note of criticism. When you say something like "You did a great job on this report, but there were quite a few typos," the "but" becomes a verbal erasure of all that came before. Save the corrective feedback for the next similar assignment.

- **As proactive**—Most of us need to work on taking the time and effort to praise more frequently. Look for opportunities to praise whenever there is positive news such as in staff meetings; use praising tools such as thank you note cards, voicemail or your notations on your planning calendar. Lead with positive and "catching people doing things right" or else you will tend to be reactive and primarily focus on mistakes in your interactions with others.

These elements of praise simply say: 1) I saw what you did, 2) I appreciate it, 3) here's why it's important and, 4) here's how it makes me feel. You can praise an employee directly or in front of others. You can even praise someone when they are not around, knowing that your remarks will more than likely make their way back to the person.

Rewards Don't Have to Be Expensive

Showing appreciation sends the message that employees are valued, and that the company or business wouldn't be able to operate without them. Involving employees in the process promotes a sense of teamwork and helpfulness. That approach is what helped Core Creative in Milwaukee become recognized by *The Business Journal* as one of the "Best Places to Work." At the end of every summer, the company sets aside time to find some creative way in which to recognize exceptional employees. From those who are simply performing well, to those who have gone above and beyond for clients, employees are celebrated and rewarded. Another company in the Midwest consistently distributes personal notes from vice presidents and managers as well as feature articles on the intranet highlighting outstanding employees. Many such effective recognition and reward items have little or no cost, as do these:

- Thank each employee personally for his or her hard work.

- Keep five coins in your packet, transfering one to another pocket each time you praise someone at work. Try to transfer all five coins each day.

- List your direct reports on your weekly "to do" list and check each name off when that person has met or exceeded expectations.

- Conduct morning chat sessions to update employees on the status of projects and to highlight desired performance by team members.

- Hold weekly team lunches so employees can share with co-workers and managers their ideas on how things are going.

A Day at the Spa

Rather than issue bonuses, the owner of Swanky Bubbles Restaurant and Champagne Bar in Philadelphia gave his employees gift cards to an upscale spa and salon. He saved thousands of dollars, and employees still felt rewarded. Employees also had the opportunity to spend time together outside of work—something many simply aren't able to do—which resulted in a greater sense of teamwork and camaraderie.

- Write about employees' accomplishments in the company newsletter or electronic bulletin board.

- Institute and encourage an open-door policy from lower level workers to management at the top. Encourage employees to talk about their concerns and their ideas for new approaches.

- Above all else, management must treat employees with trust and respect.

Sometimes, the money simply isn't there for cash rewards or high-dollar items. That doesn't mean that there aren't still options for showing employees that their time and work is valued and appreciated. Even something as simple as an ice cream social, company sponsored lunch on site, or donuts in the morning can make employees feel valued, especially when those things are in response to a job well done or individual or group achievements of some type.

Here are a few categories to consider when you next want to thank your employees:

- **Low-end Rewards**—This can include items like e-cards from Starbucks, Amazon.com, gas cards, car wash or discount restaurant coupons, gift certificates, "point" systems that can be used to purchase merchandise, a pizza, donuts or even a bouquet of flowers.

- **Symbolic Recognition**—This can be tokens, pins, ribbons, a certificate or plaque that has special meaning. For example, Busch Gardens in Tampa, Florida, supplies tokens to all supervisors to give to employees to reinforce core values. The tokens can be redeemed in the employees' paychecks for $10, but most employees who receive them prefer to keep the token and forgo the money.

- **Time Off**—Time can be used as an award itself, e.g., a voucher for a long lunch, an afternoon or an additional day off. At Greenough Communications in Boston, MA, for example, high-performing employees are awarded by being able to leave at 3 pm on Friday. And JS Communications in Los Angeles, CA, recently gave employees two free "I Don't Want to Get Out of Bed" days to use in the forthcoming year.

- **Employee Perks**—Simple low-cost benefits that are available to all employees such as soft drinks, coffee, bottled water, snacks or the use of a company fitness room great for company morale. Best, Best and Krieger has held fast to simple employee perks such as "Bagel and Donut Friday" and has retained the holiday party during tough financial times as a way to bring employees together in a social setting. And employees at Kiner Communications, a public relations firm, still enjoy baskets of fresh fruit, attend a company-sponsored Holiday party, and don't miss out on bonuses.

Peer-Initiated Recognition is Powerful

All employees like to be recognized for a job well done, but recognition from one's peers always has a special significance. Perhaps this is because such awards are seldom expected. Perhaps it is also because everyone knows managerial favoritism played no part in the selection. Whatever the reason, you can be assured that for employees to select someone from their ranks to single out for recognition and praise, that the recognition is well earned and sincere.

An example of a peer-initiated reward is described by Tom Tate, Program Manager for the Office of Personnel Management in the Personnel and Management Training Division of the U.S. Government. He tells about the "Wingspread Award," a beautiful plaque engraved and given to the division's "special performer" by the division head. After a while the recipient wanted to recognize in turn someone who they felt was a deserving colleague. The employee passed the award on to that employee who later wanted to recognize yet another peer. Over time, the award took on great value and prestige because it came from one's peers. Each employee who received it could keep it as long as he or she liked until another special performer had been discovered. When a recipient was ready to pass it on, a ceremony and lunch was scheduled. Other examples of peer-initiated awards include:

- The Angus Barn Restaurant in Raleigh, NC, has an award voted on by fellow employees called "The People's Choice" for employees who they think is a model employee, the best team player, and so forth.

- At ICI Pharmaceuticals Group in Wilmington DE, a peer can nominate a fellow employee for the "Performance Excellence Award" for any idea that helps the business (saves money, increases productivity, etc.) or for employees who go "above and beyond" the call of duty. Besides the recognition and visibility, the recipient is given $300.

- At Meridian Travel Inc. in Cleveland, OH, CEO Cynthia Bender has the company's 62 employees write in their vote for who should be Employee of the Month. "Managers always have their favorites, but the employees know who pitches in and helps out," says Bender. "This makes employees notice others more and develops camaraderie."

Getting employees to recognize other employees can be easily encouraged, but it is most likely to happen if a program is initiated in your workplace. At the Ken Blanchard Companies, in Escondido, CA, employees use the Eagle

---

Disney Does it Right Even When Busy

One of the biggest challenges in recognizing others is doing it in the midst of the daily operations of your business, that is, when you—and your employees—are the busiest. The Walt Disney World Dolphin Resort in Orlando, Florida, is an excellent example of how to provide recognition under pressure. Instead of viewing "being busy" as an executive excuse for why they didn't recognize employees, managers focus their energies on new and creative ways to do more recognition. For example:

- When surveyed, Dolphin employees reported that managers weren't around much when things were busiest. As a result, management initiated "Five-Minute Chats" where all managers were assigned 10 employees who didn't report to them. Their assignment: to check in with each employee for five minutes over the next 30 days.

- During busy days—when employees simultaneously checked in and out over 1,000 people—supervisors set up refreshments and balloons in the employee area behind the hotel check-in counter. Supervisors were there to cheer employees on and to jump in during employee breaks.

- Dolphin management started using "Wow!" cards, tri-folded wallet cards made from different colored construction paper in which employees and managers could provide a quick written thank you to others who have "wowed" a customer or another employee. "Captain Wow," their very own superhero, dropped by regularly to thank them and acknowledge their work.

No matter what your business, look for the times when you and your employees are most under pressure and develop ways to thank, acknowledge and recognize employees during those times. Doing so can be the best pressure-relief valve you'll ever have.

Award to recognize other employees for acts of extraordinary service. Anytime someone performs a work-related favor, you can give them a "hatchling," a foil sticker of an egg plus a write up about what they did and why it was of special significance to you.

Once an employee receives 16 hatchlings they are given an Eagle Award plaque by a group of employees in a brief ceremony at his or her desk accompanied by a photo, balloons, etc. An Eagle Award can also be given for a single outstanding event an employee performs. The program was announced and explained at a company meeting and a small committee of volunteers administers the mechanics of the program. Employee reception to the program has been strong. The program evolved to the creation of "People's Choice" awards that were customized, hand-made awards created by employees for other employees, which added fun and meaning to the recognition activity.

Involve Employees in Acts of Recognition

Encourage employees to recognize their co-workers for an exceptional job or for going above and beyond their normal responsibilities. Create certificates or notes that co-workers can give to each other and have the managers of awarded employees include a personal note or token of appreciation. Or, create a simple newsletter or weekly update to recognize employees and call attention to top performers. Establish a system where employees nominate their top co-workers each week. The result is camaraderie and teamwork among employees, as well as increased job satisfaction.

Rewarding Employees as a Team

Group recognition and rewards are also important. In fact, if you do not reinforce team successes, it will be difficult to get continued teamwork from your group.

Teambuilding activities can serve a dual purpose. First, they help unite employees and create an improved sense of community. Second, they can be a nice break from the monotony of work, something that is much needed in a downtime when morale and spirits are low. As an added benefit to the company

---

Keys to Successful Teambuilding

- Understand your employees—know what they want and need and where they could use improvements
- Ensure that managers spend time with employees to connect with them on a professional and personal level
- Encourage successful managers to share with co-workers how they motivate and connect with their employees
- Develop an activity or program that encourages continued work as a team throughout the remainder of the year

---

and employees alike, such activities promote working together by creating a more positive atmosphere wherein employees tend to work harder and more efficiently. Some effective teambuilding exercises include:

- Trust building games
- Wilderness adventures
- Scavenger hunts
- Cooking classes

Teambuilding With a Twist

After General Mills acquired Pillsbury, division leaders came together and organized the Spirit Team. The sole purpose of this group was to organize activities that brought everyone together and sparked positive attitudes. The Spirit Team organized volunteer days at a nonprofit organization, building on the idea that teambuilding cannot be fully accomplished with just one event. Now, the group organizes between eight and ten events at the same organization each year. The result has been positive feedback on employee surveys citing a connection to the volunteer program and their good feelings about their jobs as well as the company.

A Sense of Sharing at Shared Technologies, Inc.

Shared Technologies in Coppell, Texas has an Employee Support Fund that is available to employees if they are struggling financially. The Fund, which was established by CEO Tony Parella, was developed not only to help employees, but to encourage and increase a team atmosphere. Parella, who is known among workers at all 20 branches of the company as always being there for his employees, published a book about how he turned the company around. Half of the sales from the book went directly to the Employee Support Fund. Surveys regarding employee's thoughts on Parella were distributed to his workers before the book was published and elicited responses so positive that each and every one was published in the book.

Summary

What is the best way to motivate employees in tough times? Surveys, studies and discussions with employees from all walks of life in all industries have revealed a very simple formula for successfully rewarding employees: Treat your employees with respect, pay them fairly, and notice, recognize and reward them when they do a good job.

Although money is a motivator, it is not the only motivator, and it does have its limitations. Often, simple, creative, no-cost ways to show your appreciation in a timely way can have a larger impact on your employees in making them feel special and motivating them to rise to the occasion in difficult times.

You should recognize employees for both their progress toward an achievement of desired performance goals and show appreciation for the small accomplishments as well as the big ones. The recognition must be ongoing to reinforce employees' need to feel that they're doing a good job. Recognition and rewards should be given to individuals and groups alike, as deserved.

Seven Important Lessons of Motivating Employees

1. **You get what you reward.** Be sure you have clearly defined what you want to get, then use rewards and recognition to move toward those goals.

2. **What motivates people, motivates people.** What is motivating to individuals varies from person to person. To be on target, ask employees what they want.

3. **The most motivating rewards take little or no money.** Try a sincere thank you, providing information, involving employees in decision making—especially as it affects them.

4. **Everyone wants to be appreciated.** Competent people, quiet people, and even managers want to know that what they are doing is important and meaningful.

5. **All behavior is controlled by its consequences.** Positive consequences will most quickly lead to desired behavior and enhanced performance.

6. **Management is what you do with people, not to them.** Tell employees what you want to do and why. By involving them, you'll more easily gain their commitment and support.

7. **Common sense is often not common practice.** It's not what you believe or say—it's what you do. Practice recognizing people and their achievements on a daily basis.

CONCLUSION

T his book has been organized around a few of the most proven principles of performance management and my original research as to what most motivates employees today when they do a good job at work, supported by current examples of what the best companies do to motivate their employees to get results in tough times.

Most of the techniques and examples presented were simple, easy to implement, and required little if any budget, and all of them produced positive results. Ironically, those things which have the greatest value in driving desired results in the workplace today are increasingly more intangible, informal and interpersonal (e.g., praise, involvement, support) as opposed to things that are more tangible, formal and program-driven (e.g., raises, awards, banquets).

The means and frequency of communication is especially important in tough times and comes in many forms. Whether it's a business update of sales prospects, a brainstorming session on possible solutions to a problem or a simple thank you note for a job well done, communication is by far one of the most important aspects of any manager's job for inspiring performance and motivation.

In challenging times, managers must tap into the talents, interests and skills of their employees in order to get the best they have to offer the organization. Getting to know employees on a personal level and asking them for their input, help and ideas is a great starting point for any manager.

In most cases, giving employees the autonomy and authority to act in the best interests of the organization and offering encouragement and praise along the way works wonders. Encouraging employees to pursue their ideas and supporting them in that process is also important for yielding positive results in the workplace.

In today's fast-paced, ever-changing, technology-driven world of business, employees are increasingly expected to be responsible for their own work and take greater initiative in their jobs. Managers have had to change the ways in which they lead—moving from an authoritarian "command and control" model to one of greater employee support and encouragement.

All the strategies discussed in this book represent good management practices, which are important in good times but can mean the difference between success and failure for any company in tough times. As times improve, these strategies should continue to serve you and your organization well.

Downtimes often serve as a perfect catalyst for change. When resources are plentiful, there is little need to be creative, frugal or efficient. As such, it's much more difficult to implement changes and improvements when nothing appears to be broken. Weathering this economic storm by making smart and effective changes can not only help you survive this economic crisis, it can make you better prepared when the current crisis ends.

Getting Results in Tough Times: A Summary

All performance starts with clear goals and expectations. Set a compelling direction for all employees and revise goals accordingly.

The most important aspect for building morale and engaging employees in tough times is open and honest communication. Communicate clearly, frequently and at a personal level.

Every employee has a $50,000 idea. Ask for employee ideas, suggestions and feedback for how things could be improved on an ongoing basis. Organize teams to explore possibilities.

Involve employees in decision making, especially on those matters that directly affect them and their jobs. This increases employee buy-in and commitment.

Provide employees with adequate autonomy, flexibility and support to get the job done. Be assessible. Help employees when they need it, as they need it.

Work is becoming a state of mind more than a place to be. Allow employees flexibility in how they get their work done and in their working hours.

Get to know employees well, establish open relationships and accessibility.

Realize that most development is self-development and occurs on the job with the opportunities that job already provides.

Identify opportunities where employees can contribute more to the success of the organization. Align those development opportunities with the skills and interests of your employees, providing training as needed to succeed.

You get what you recognize and reward. Be sure to notice people when they have excelled and thank them in sincere and meaningful ways. A simple thanks or note of appreciation can go a long way.

Celebrate successes when those successes occur in fun and public ways.

Pay people fairly but treat them superbly when they do good work.

RELATED ARTICLES
BY BOB NELSON

The Ultimate Expectation

An essential part of any manager's job is inspiring employees to go beyond their job descriptions to do what needs to be done without waiting to be told to do it. I call this "The Ultimate Expectation" and it includes such activities as:

- Serving a customer
- Solving a problem
- Assisting a co-worker
- Suggesting a cost-saving idea
- Developing a recommendation
- Improving a process or
- Volunteering to take on an additional assignment or responsibility

I created an open letter to employees that explains the concept that you can share with your employees when they are first hired:

Dear Employee:

You've been hired to handle some pressing needs we have. If we could have gotten by in not hiring you, we would have. But we've determined that we needed someone with your skills and experience and that you were the best person to help us with our needs. We have offered you the position and you've accepted. Thanks!

During the course of your employment, you will be asked to do many things: general responsibilities, specific assignments, group and individual projects. You will have many chances to excel and to confirm that we made a good choice in hiring you.

However, there is one foremost responsibility that may never be specifically requested of you, but that you need to always keep in mind through the duration of your employment. This is The Ultimate Expectation and it is as follows:

Always do what most needs to be done
without waiting to be asked.

We've hired you to do a job, yes, but more important, we've hired you to think and act in the best interests of the organization at all times. If we never say this again, don't take it as an indication that it's no longer important or that we've changed our priorities. We are likely to get caught up in the daily press of business, the never-ending changes of the operation, and the rush of activities. This may make it look like this principle no longer applies. Don't be deceived by this.

As long as you are employed with us, you have our permission to act in our mutual best interests. If at any time you do not feel we are doing the right thing—the thing you most believe would help us all—please say so. You have our permission to speak up when necessary to state what is unstated, to make a suggestion, or to question an action or decision.

This doesn't mean we will always agree with you, nor that we will necessarily change what we are doing; but we always want to hear what you most believe would help us better achieve our goals and purpose and to create a mutually successful experience in the process.

You will need to seek to understand how (and why) things are done the way they are done, before you seek to change existing work processes. Try to work with the systems that are in place, but tell us if you think those systems need to be changed.

Discuss what is presented here with me and others in the organization so that we might all get better at applying The Ultimate Expectation.

Sincerely,

Your Manager

p.s.: Like much sound advice, The Ultimate Expectation seems like common sense. Don't confuse what sounds simple with what is easy to do. Take this message to heart and become skilled at applying it to your own job and circumstances. Once you learn The Ultimate Expectation, you can apply it every day to your work. Accepting this challenge is paramount to your success in your job, in your career, and even in your life.

Being able to fulfill the Ultimate Expectation is a virtue every worker possesses, but few seem to demonstrate. It can be an essential element for helping any organization thrive—especially in tough times.

Here are some further suggestions you can make to employees to help them see the difference they can make at work:

- **Think about how things could be improved.** Make at least two suggestions a week in your job—and act on those suggestions.

- **Ask silly questions.** Even if it sounds silly at the time, a simple question can lead to new and better approaches. The question you ask may have never been asked before; or, if it was, perhaps the timing has changed and question is now more relevant and viable.

- **Turn needs into opportunities.** Learn to look at the customer's needs and ask how you might better satisfy those needs. Look at the organization's needs and ask how those needs might be creatively addressed.

- **Make your job more difficult.** Take on work, volunteer to help others, and ask to be on projects or teams created to address pressing problems or to capitalize on opportunities.

Employees who fulfill The Ultimate Expectation make a valuable contribution to their organizations—and, in the process, take control of their careers. In today's workplace, no one can afford to be just average. Even in the toughest of times, employees can be in charge of their own destiny by being proactive about what they do to make a difference in their jobs today.

For more information and ideas about how employees can exceed expectations at work, see *Please Don't Just Do What I Tell You: Do What Needs to Be Done!* **by Bob Nelson, Ph.D.**

Inspiring Employees to Take Initiative at Work

One of the biggest mistakes employees can make in life is to think that they work for someone else. True, all employees have a boss and they collect a paycheck where they work, but ultimately they are master of their own destinies. It's up to them to decide what potential they reach in their careers and what they will accomplish in their lives. Every day they have the chance to excel, to be exceptional, and to make a difference where they work.

Every manager has the ability—and the responsibility—to tap into the potential of their employees, to inspire them to be their best, and to show them the possibilities of what they can achieve at work. A fundamental aspect of this responsibility is helping employees see the connection between their jobs and the mission and purpose of the organization so that they can act in ways that best serve the organization on a day-to-day basis. I refer to these independent actions employees take as initiative.

Employees who take initiative to go beyond the status quo are the lifeblood of every successful organization. Taking initiative is a key ingredient in making improvements at work, dealing with change, and providing superior customer service. It is also one of the best ways employees can advance their careers.

In an online survey conducted by iVillage.com, employees were asked, "What is most important for getting ahead in the workplace?" Of the 7,760 people who cast their vote, some 55 percent said that "initiative" is most important, followed by the attributes of "inspiration" with 17 percent of the vote, "intelligence" with 16 percent, and "political savvy" with 12 percent.

"Taking initiative" can mean many things for employees: tapping their inner creativity, tackling a persistent problem, capitalizing on opportunities, or creating ways to improve their current work environment. By taking initiative in any of these ways, employees can elevate their visibility in the organization and greatly enhance their chances for recognition, learning, advancement, and financial rewards.

All employees have the skills needed to take initiative at work—they just might not be aware of those capabilities. By helping employees understand and explore the concept of initiative, focusing on what they *can* do, and emphasizing possibilities within their *own* sphere of influence, managers can help employees have a greater impact at work.

Here, then, are six specific skills and strategies that managers can help employees develop to better take initiative at work:

Skills #1: Being a Self-Leader

Self-leadership is the essence of initiative; it's having employees themselves be in charge of their work without constant intervention and monitoring by their manager. It is also getting employees to make decisions themselves instead of waiting for their managers to make decisions for them. What happens when employees are self-leaders? In a recent survey of senior managers, direct employee involvement in decision making, including taking initiative, was cited as the major factor in increased productivity over a recent five-year period.

While managers use policies, procedures, milestones and directives to push employees to achieve the goals of the organization, leaders inspire their associates to achieve the goals of the organization through their actions and example. To be a leader one needs a vision of the way things should be, the passion to convince others to join in, and the initiative to get started. For example:

Several years ago, John Patrick, a senior strategy executive with IBM in Somers, NY, realized that the Internet would be the future of computing. Soon after his net conversion, Patrick acted independently and quickly. He wrote an IBM internal manifesto called "Get Connected." It identified a number of principles that would reshape industries and reinvent companies, along with the following action items:

- Give every employee an e-mail address.
- Create internal newsgroups.
- Build a corporate website.

Patrick immediately began to receive memos, phone calls, and email from around the world. Says Patrick, "People didn't know where I reported in the company and they didn't care. We shared a common vision that the Internet was going to change everything and that IBM should be a leader." When IBM created a 600-person division to define the company's Internet initiatives a couple of years later, Patrick was named its vice president and chief technology officer.

Leaders influence actions...

Encourage employees to:

- Seek positions of leadership, both formal and informal.
- Set an example.
- Become a valuable resource.
- Be prepared when they present their case.
- Stick to the facts, not emotion.

For initiative to have an impact throughout an organization, communicating effectively with others is essential. According to Cheryl Babcock of Sarasota, FL, her ability to communicate well with her colleagues is part of her success in helping nudge her organization out of the tired, old ways of doing business, and into new, more effective ones. As she described it:

"I'm a change agent because I'm willing to spend my time talking, writing, emailing, and so on to make other people aware of the paradigm shift that's taking place in my field. I don't always get paid for the time I spend doing that, but I do it anyway. I'll actually go out of my way to do it because I believe so strongly in the process. To be a change agent employees need both the ability to talk (in a variety of mediums) so people will at least hear what they are saying and the ability to enlist others to promote the cause. The other thing is passion—if they don't have it, nobody else will 'catch' it."

Managers can encourage employees to be leaders by drawing them out, listening to and encouraging their ideas and giving them permission to proceed in developing and implementing those ideas. Managers can be on the look out for development opportunities when assigning tasks, projects and responsibilities to employees that show leadership promise through their interest, ambitions and past performance. Managers can also hold development discussions with employees to give them feedback about what they are good at and where they could improve in their jobs and skills they could develop. Managers should also periodically hold career discussions with each of their employees about various options and career paths the employee might consider.

Skill #2: Positive Accountability

Employees who take initiative at work have a positive belief and accountability that they can make a difference. They don't settle for the norm—they think outside the box. Innovation is the spark that keeps organizations moving ever onward and upward. Employees can innovate to (1) improve products and services, (2) find a new way to do something, (3) make a task easier or a process faster, (4) save money, (5) enhance their jobs, and (6) increase their promotability. Without innovation, new products and services, new ways of doing business would never emerge. Some examples:

One day, Rich Coutchie, an engineer at Lorin Industries, and anodized-aluminum products manufacturer in Muskegon, MI, was handling a computer disk just like the millions of others in use around the world every day. He looked at the shutter door on the disk, which was then made of stainless steel, and asked himself, "Why couldn't this shutter be made of anodized aluminum?" Good question. If it *could* be made of anodized aluminum, his idea would open up a huge new market for his company. And, because Lorin Industries is a Scanlon participative management company—committed to the principles of employee involvement—management listened to Coutchie's idea, and ultimately approved it. The impact of his idea for Lorin Industries included the building of an entirely new production line to anodize the aluminum for this product, which led to a 42 percent increase in sales.

Several years ago, when the office of Amy's Ice Cream in Austin, TX, happened to run out of job application forms, a quick-thinking employee handed each remaining applicant an empty bag with instructions to do something creative with it. Because Amy's strives to hire people who can entertain customers, this brainstorm allowed applicants to demonstrate their ability right then and there. One particularly ingenious applicant transformed her bag into a helium-filled balloon and floated it into the interview area. (She got the job.) The bags quickly became a standard for the interview process.

Employees who take initiative think differently. They...

- Look for new combinations.
- Ask "what if?" or develop "what-if" scenarios.
- Consider approaches they've never thought about before.
- Brainstorm with others.
- Become champions of new ideas.

One of the easiest, and most effective, ways for employees to take initiative is to have a mindset for making suggestions, that is, being on the lookout for ways to improve the work processes, services, and systems that are a vital part of how the organization conducts business. No organization is perfect; there is always room for improvement and for new approaches to old problems. If there is ever a place where anyone in an organization can take initiative, it's with making a suggestion to improve something.

Everyone can make significant contributions to the organization—ones that will help the organization and bring them personal satisfaction, as well. For example:

When a staffer at Dana Corporation got wind of the company's plan to build additional parking lots at its plant in Elizabethtown, KY, at an estimated cost of $110,000, he was convinced that there must be a better solution. On his own, the staffer decided to come up with an alternative plan of action that would solve the problem but that would not cost the company a dime. His idea was to slightly stagger work schedules at the three-shift plant, and management gladly implemented it. The new parking spaces instantly became unnecessary, and Dana Corporation was able to direct its financial resources to more pressing needs.

While working for Berkeley Challenge, a cleaning company in Brisbane, Australia, crew leader Alison Phillipe had long wondered how to make the process of cleaning the Brisbane Entertainment Centre, a large sports and entertainment facility, more efficient and cost-effective. Her lead employee, Peter Thistlethwaite, asked if he could try organizing a better way to get the job done. A week after Phillipe said yes, Thistlethwaite came back with an organized method of cleaning the seating arena that decreased labor cost by almost 15 percent. Not only that, but the quality of the work improved and the staff's motivation increased as employees actively sought to give their own input about how to improve the cleaning process. Says Phillipe, "I was impressed by the change that I eventually left the company and returned to school to learn how to manage people properly and effectively."

Managers can encourage employees to consistently be thinking of and suggest new ideas, strategies and recommendations, For example, by having them list a number of possible solutions to a problem rather than just pursuing the initial solution they think of. Managers can and should ask all employees for their opinions and ideas on a frequent basis, encouraging them to meet with others to brainstorm and develop their ideas.

How to make their suggestions count...

Start in their own areas. Employees can have the most impact in the area they know the most about. In their current job, look for ways to save money, improve service, or streamlines processes. Experiment as necessary to test their ideas.

Develop a mindset for making suggestions. Have employees get in the habit of thinking about potential improvements throughout the day, such as while they are commuting to work. Have them carry a notepad with them and jot ideas down. Try to develop a minimum of two ideas per week that they can submit or share with others.

Support and build on the suggestions of others. By supporting other people's ideas, employees will develop good will and alliances that can be beneficial when they need help and support.

Have an implementation plan. Suggestions can sound like complaints if there is no plan to implement them. Employees can think through the costs and benefits of their ideas and how they can make—or initiate—the proposed change. Document the idea and share it with others. Determine who else would need to be involved to implement the suggestion and solicit their input, involvement and approval early on. "Own" their ideas and see those suggestions through to fruition.

Skill #3: Planning and Preparation

As most successful professionals realize, preparation is often the key to success in any endeavor. It's not good enough to have a good idea, employees need to think their ideas through. Doing the necessary preparation to support an idea or recommendation, such as: research on the Internet, tracking the number of occurrences of a problem or complaint, or determining the financial savings if a problem was corrected. For example:

When Patrick Sinner at PNC bank of Pittsburgh, PA, came up with the energy-saving idea of requiring employees to turn off their computers at the end of each workday, management objected, citing a commonly held, but erroneous belief that regularly switching the computer on and off would dramatically shorten its life. However, Sinner did not quit there. He further investigated the topic and came up with the research studies that supported his belief. When Sinner presented these studies to management, thus proving that the computers would be retired long before any negative impact of all the on-and-off switching would show on the equipment, management finally agreed. The resulting energy savings amounted to $268,000 per year.

Beverly Scibilia of United Electronic Controls in Watertown, MA, had the complex and strenuous job of assembling temperature controls for large hospital sterilizers. Knowing there must be a way to reduce the amount of time and effort required to compete the process, she pulled together a group of co-workers to watch her use the large, heavy press and then offer ideas on how to improve the process. Scibilia took their suggestions and worked with the model shop to design a new machine. What used to take an hour now takes no more than 15 minutes. Another machine, which works on the same principle, reduced setup time from 45 minutes to a matter of seconds. According to Scibilia, the time it takes for her to get out an order now is just a fraction of what it was before. "What took me six weeks before, I can now get out in a week."

A Problem Solving Process

Solving problems is often the reason why managers want employees to take initiative in the first place. Here are some suggestions for your employees for solving problems in a systematic way:

1. **Define the problem.** Is there really a problem? If so, determine exactly what it is, how big it is, and if it is going to continue to be a problem in the future.

2. **Gather data.** Before they start looking for solutions to the problem, gather as much data about it as they possible can without unduly delaying their efforts.

3. **Consider alternate solutions to the problem.** Make a list of the most likely solutions to the problem and prioritize them from most to least likely.

4. **Pick the best solution.** Choose the most likely solution at the top of their list. Be ready to proceed to the next solution if their choice does not generate the results they seek.

5. **Apply the best solution.** Put their most likely solutions into action. Closely monitor the results to see if it solves their problem. If so, congratulations! They can move on to the next problem. If not, apply the next most likely solution.

J. Douglas Phillips, senior director of corporate planning at Merck Headquarters in White House Station, NJ, uses cost studies of employee turnover to justify the company's investments in work and family benefits. The research he does before he presents his proposals to management pays off in a big way. According to Phillips, such bottomline demonstrations add to his internal credibility in promoting such programs as day-care centers and lunchtime employee forums on teenage drug abuse.

Managers can help employees develop their ideas by serving as a sounding board to listen to employees, helping them to brainstorm ways they can obtain supporting data, encouraging them to interview or discuss their ideas with others in the organization or to benchmark related best practices with other companies.

Skill #4: Presentation and Sales

Almost always, taking initiative requires that employees convince others to support their point of view and to buy into their suggestions. Here are some tips for helping employees present their ideas to others:

- **Outline their goals.** What are they trying to accomplish? Do they want to convince their boss to try a new approach to solve a customer service problem? Perhaps they'd like to form a committee to develop ways to improve the environmental friendliness of their organization? Have them first outline their goals in writing, and then hone them before they present those goals to their target audience.

- **Develop a list of the positive points of their plan.** Decide on the key advantages of using their ideas and collect data—both qualitative and quantitative—that support their plan. These major points will form the backbone of their presentation.

- **Do a negative-objection analysis.** Have employees think through the questions and objections their proposal is likely to receive. Develop a sound response for each and have them collect additional data and evidence they need to address any question or objection.

- **Presell their idea.** Informally approach others whose opinions they respect to get their feedback on their proposals. Not only will they find ways to improve their plan, but those who are involved in the review process will be more apt to buy into the proposal.

When Jenny Cutler, a programmer for a Silicon Valley firm, visited her mother-in-law in the hospital, she had a terrific idea for a new medical product that could be developed relatively easily by modifying one of her company's current products. Cutler asked both her boss and her boss's boss to meet with her about the idea. Impressed with Cutler's concept, proposal and presentation, they approved the development of the new product, and she was authorized to spend up to half of her time developing a prototype and creating a financial forecast of its viability.

Kelly McGovern, former vice president of Internet/telecommunications at Bay Networks, a computer networking firm in Billerica, MA, was instrumental in convincing top management to extend the company's benefits program to domestic partners, despite an initial response that was lukewarm, at best. How did she do it? "I went around the roadblocks," says McGovern, "and I found someone to help me champion my cause." In this case, her champion was incoming company president David House. He read a copy of a business analysis that McGovern researched and prepared showing that extending benefits to domestic partners would cost Bay Networks relatively little, but that the upside in terms of improved employee morale, retention, and performance, would be tremendous. House agreed with her analysis, and the program was immediately put into effect.

Managers can help employees better present and sell their ideas to others by listening to a dry run of an employee's proposal, asking questions and raising predictable objections that will likely arise.

Skill #5: Perseverance and Persistence

If there are heroes among those employees who choose to take initiative on the job, their stories are usually ones of extraordinary perseverance and persistence against entrenched policies and systems that work to ensure the status quo. It often takes a fair amount of guts to take initiative in the first place. But to persist—even when an employee seems defeated or, worse, when they've been directed to no longer pursue their idea—takes an incredible amount of fortitude.

Soon after Yumi started in an entry-level position at a Hitachi silicon-wafer fabrication plant in Japan, she learned that management was reviewing a proposal to close the plant because of a defect rate that was some 20 percent higher than the norm. Riding to work one day on her bike, Yumi noticed that a passing train caused her handlebars to vibrate. Armed with this discovery, she suggested to the plant manager that perhaps there was a link between the high defect rate and passing trains. Although skeptical about Yumi's theory, he passed her idea on to Hitachi's corporate quality engineers, who conducted vibration tests, but came up empty-handed. Yumi did not lose faith in her idea. She did more research and discovered that some low-frequency vibrations could escape detection, but still have a negative effect. Yumi convinced management to try building a moat filled with water between the train tracks and the plant. A group of employee volunteers took on the project one weekend. To almost everyone's surprise, the idea worked and the plant was saved from being closed.

Persistence pays off...

Help employees to:

- Focus on what they can do, not on what they cannot do.
- Not give up, especially if they truly believe in their idea, suggestion or proposal.
- Look for ways to get others to say "yes."
- Identify roadblocks to their goals and then dismantle those objections, one by one.
- Be assertive, not aggressive. Be polite, but persistent.

Hewlett-Packard engineer Charles House was given a medal for "extraordinary contempt and defiance beyond the normal call of engineering duty." Why? He had ignored an order from company founder David Packard to stop working on a type of high-quality video monitor. Despite the rebuke, House pressed ahead and succeeded in developing the monitor, which was used to track NASA's manned moon landings and is also now used in heart transplants. Although early estimates indicated that the market for such large-screen displays would be only 30 units, more than 17,000 of them—worth about $35 million—were sold.

Emily Rodriquez, corporate director of transportation for Esprit de Corp, a San Francisco-based clothing manufacturer, was convinced that consolidating overseas product orders into fewer but larger shipments was necessary for Esprit to control its imports. When she first submitted a proposal to the vice president of operations, it was buried. Undaunted, she maintained up-to-date information supporting her contention. One year later, when it was apparent to upper management that something had to be done, she was able to immediately provide fresh information to augment the year-old proposal. She was on the next plane to Asia with authority to implement her recommendation.

Managers can help encourage employees to be persistent by being excited about employee efforts, open and supportive when they are stuck or need your help, consoling to employees reach an impasse, yet constructive in helping them consider new options for moving their ideas forward.

Employees who take initiative learn from their mistakes. They...

- Are able to identify their mistakes.
- Ask themselves what could have been done differently.
- Plan to apply what they have learned in future situations.

Skill #6: Managing Up

The traditional view of "management" brings to mind visions of bosses dictating orders down to their subordinates. However, management isn't limited to this old-fashioned view of how to get things done in an organization. Workers can push their own innovative ideas, opinions, and decisions up the organization as well and help their managers do a better job and to improve the performance of their organizations in the process. Every organization needs this effort from employees at all levels of the organization. In one study conducted by Sydney Yoshiba for Ford Motor Company's British Columbia division found that senior management could identify only 4 percent of the problems in an organization, but when middle management, all supervisors, and all staff were factored in, this proportion increased to 9 percent, 74 percent, and 100 percent, respectively.

Secrets to managing up...

- **Make your boss look good.** They better job your boss does, the better the department—and the boss—will look to corporate higher-ups.

- **Don't be shy.** Tell your boss what's on your mind—don't make him or her guess.

- **Be proactive.** Anticipate problems and solve those problems when small, before the problems become bigger and require more time, resources and energy on everyone's part.

- **Be your own best advocate.** Learn how to present a clear and compelling case for what you want. Support your case with facts and evidence, not speculation and emotion.

- **Enlist others to help.** There is strength in numbers. The more people you can bring around to your point of view, the better chance you'll have of implementing your idea or recommendation.

Employees who take initiative realize that empathy plays a big part in their ability to effectively manage up. Keeping in mind that their boss may be under more stress and pressure from above, and below, than they realize. A sincere, specific, and timely message that says employees appreciate a particular behavior on the part of managers goes a long way toward reinforcing the very behavior they value—making for a better workplace for everyone. Employees who master the skill of managing up will have much greater control over their own destiny—both on and off the job.

Bill Taylor, regional team leader for CP Corporation in San Jose, CA, had a new employee tell him: "Once a month I'm going to come into your office and tell you about all the great things I've been doing. You're going to agree with me because I need to hear that from you." Taylor agreed, and after about six months, at the end of one such meeting, the employee announced: "You're getting good at this!" Taylor had to agree, because he never took time to thank or praise employees before.

According to Marsha Shade, administrative assistant at Baudville, Inc., a producer of team-building software, papers, and accessories, located in Grand Rapids, MI, one way employees can determine what ideas and solutions to push up the organization to management is to "pretend" that the company or business they are working for belongs to them. The difference in perspective that comes from a "the-company-belongs-to-me" attitude encourages each employee to see him- or herself as crucial to the success of the business. Self-motivating thoughts like "If I owned this company I would…" or "If I was in charge I could…" can lead an employee to research a project or task and make constructive suggestions for change. Thinking and acting as if "the company belongs to me" encourages employees to consider the "big picture," dream big, a and to think beyond his or her own area of the business. If "the company belongs to me" as an employee, they have much to gain by making sure the ways they do their jobs help the organization to succeed.

When John Rogener, program director for Citicorp/Citibank's transaction services training department, was directed by management to train 1,700 employees in object-oriented technology, he sensed that the training would not be effective; the employees would not learn the things that they needed to get their jobs done. Rogener came up with what he considered a better way and presented it up the organizational chain of command. Instead of training 1,700 employees all at once, he convinced management to support his plan for varied and smaller-scale training. Says Rogener, "What's the bottom line? You have to believe in yourself. You must be responsible for your own decisions rather than let the institution dictate to you."

Ashley Korenblat, former president of Merlin Manufacturing, a Cambridge, MA-based bike manufacturer, decided to redesign the rear brakes on the company's rugged road bikes. She was certain that the new design would be cheaper because it didn't involve expensive welding, and Merlin could subcontract out the work during a period in which it would otherwise be extremely busy. Korenblat gave the go-ahead to start production. Shortly after the first order was placed, her purchasing agent, realizing the new design was faulty, approached Korenblat and insisted that she reconsider her decision. Korenblat allows, "I probably wasn't very successful at disguising my impatience." After taking another look, however, it turned out that the new design was going to lead to a new series of expenses that added up to a lot more than a little extra welding time. By taking the initiative to push Korenblat to review her decision, the purchasing agent helped the company avoid a costly mistake. Says Korenblat, "I had to admit I'd been just plain wrong. That employee's persistence saved us a lot of money."

To help employees develop the skill of managing up, managers must first tell them they are open to employee feedback and suggestions for how they can be a better manager. They need to solicit feedback from their employees for how they could provide better direction, support and guidance to employees in their jobs. When such feedback is offered, managers need to thank employees for the feedback and reinforce why the information is important to them. If you have a negative reaction to the feedback, initially avoid sharing that reaction and instead find something positive you can focus on about the feedback.

Developing a strong working relationship with their boss...

Employees need to:

- Take action on potential problems before they become real problems.
- Be willing to take on new challenges.
- Resist being a "yes" man or "yes" woman.
- Avoid trying to hide bad news.
- Anticipate the needs of their organization and their boss, and act on both.

All employees can take initiative at work—if they put their minds to it. Those employees who are most successful at taking initiative become self leaders, learn to hold themselves accountable to come up with new ideas and suggestions, to research and develop those ideas, to present their recommendations to others well, and to persist and persevere when they are not initially successful. In addition, they learn to "manage up" and help their own managers be better leaders to them and to others. The skills in taking initiative are not innate; rather, these skills can be learned and perfected over time with the help of one's manager.

The biggest mistake employees can make is to think they work for someone else. Help your employees avoid this mistake by getting them to use these six skills for taking initiative in their jobs to enhance their impact for you, for them, and for the organization.

For more information and ideas on how employees can take initiative at work, see *1001 Ways to Take Initiative at Work* **by Bob Nelson, Ph.D.**

INDEX

Featured Companies

A

Accountemps, pp. 15, 34, 101
 Menlo Park, CA
Allied Steel, pp. 37–38
 Fort Lauderdale, FL
American Express, p. 85
 New York, NY
Amy's Ice Cream, p. 128
 Austin, TX
Angus Barn, p. 108
 Raleigh, NC
AT&T, p. 14
 Dallas, TX
AT&T Universal Card Services, p. 56
 Jacksonville, FL

B

Banner Health, p. 94
 Phoenix, AZ
Baudville, Inc., p. 136
 Grand Rapids, MI
Bay Networks, p. 133
 Billerica, MA
Berkeley Challenge, p. 129
 Brisbane, Australia
Best Buy, p. 38
 Richfield, MN
Best, Best and Krieger, pp. 77, 107–08
 Riverside, CA
Boardroom Inc., pp. 57–58
 Greenwich, CT

Busch Gardens, p. 107
 Tampa, FL
Business Journal, p. 106
 Milwaukee, WI
BzzAgent, p. 45
 Boston, MA

C

Champions Solutions Group, p. 59
 West Palm Beach, FL
Charles Schwab, pp. 90–91
 San Francisco, CA
Chevrolet, p. 13
 Detroit, MI
CIGNA, p. 79
 Philadelphia, PA
CitiBank, pp. 136–37
 New York, NY
ComPsych, p. 78
 Chicago, IL
Computer Science Corp., p. 40
 Falls Church, VA
Container Store, p. 87
 Coppell, TX
Core Creative, p. 106
 Milwaukee, WI
CP Corporation, pp. 55, 136
 San Jose, CA

D

Dana Corporation, p. 129
 Toledo, OH

S

T

U

V

W

ABOUT BOB NELSON

Few people have had the influence on the field of management and motivation as Dr. Bob Nelson. He is president of Nelson Motivation, Inc., a management training and consulting company located in San Diego, California that specializes in helping organizations improve their management practices, programs and systems, and has worked with or consulted for almost two-thirds of the companies on the *Fortune* 500 list. He is co-founder of Recognition Professionals International and previously worked closely with Dr. Ken Blanchard (*The One Minute Manager*) as his principal writer, co-author, chief of staff and vice president of The Ken Blanchard Companies for ten years.

As a best-selling author, Dr. Nelson has sold over 3 million business books on management and motivation, including *1001 Ways to Reward Employees* (now in its 2nd edition), *The 1001 Rewards & Recognition Fieldbook*, *1001 Ways to Energize Employees*, *1001 Ways to Take Initiative at Work*, *Managing For Dummies* (now in its 2nd edition), and *The Management Bible,* among others. His books have been translated into over 30 languages worldwide.

As a media expert, Dr. Nelson has frequently appeared in the national media including, on television: CBS "60 Minutes," CNN, MSNBC, PBS; on radio: National Public Radio, Bloomberg Radio, Business News Network, and USA Radio Network; and, in print: *The New York Times, The Wall Street Journal, The Washington Post, The Chicago Tribune, The Philadelphia Inquirer, USA Today,* and *Business Week, Fortune, Entrepreneur* and *Inc.* magazines to discuss how to best motivate today's employees. He has been a columnist for American City Business Journals, *Corporate Meetings & Incentives,* and *Bank Marketing,* among others.

As a professional speaker, Dr. Nelson has presented to over 1000 organizations as well as for numerous conferences, associations, public seminars and business groups both across the United States as well as abroad on six continents. He frequently presents webinars and satellite conferences to live audiences, some in excess of 80,000 people.

Dr. Nelson holds an MBA in organizational behavior from UC Berkeley and received his PhD in management from The Peter F. Drucker Graduate Management School at Claremont Graduate University in suburban Los Angeles, where he worked with the late Dr. Peter Drucker, "The Father of Modern Management."

OTHER BOOKS BY BOB NELSON

1001 Ways to Reward Employees, Revised Edition

Bob Nelson's best-selling book, *1001 Ways to Reward Employees* with over 1.5 million copies sold, is now available in an updated, revised edition. It features a reorganized and expanded contents (100 pages longer), based on what employees most report they want today from Bob's on-going and doctoral research at The Peter F. Drucker Graduate Management School, his work with over 1000 organizations, and new, never-before-published examples from over 300 organizations. It is a "must have" resource for every manager, small business owner, and human resources practitioner! Softback, 381 pages.

The 1001 Rewards and Recognition Fieldbook

Beginning with the basics of motivation this book lays the groundwork for developing and managing a rewards or recognition initiative in any work environment: how to recognize an individual or a group; how to develop a low-cost recognition program; how to sell rewards and recognition to upper management, prevent and fix common problems, and assess effectiveness. There are planning worksheets, templates for best practices, recognition ideas, answers to frequently asked questions, and more! Softback, 388 pages.

1001 Ways to Energize Employees

The best employee motivators often cost little or nothing and this book exemplifies how to apply motivation using the work itself, including such topics as communication techniques, empowerment, visibility, self-directed teams, suggestion systems, continuous improvement, delegation techniques and much more! Softback, 213 pages.

1001 Ways to Take Initiative at Work

This is the first management book for employees. Weaving together case studies, examples, quotes, research highlights, and the author's own "Tool Box" of management techniques and exercises, this practical handbook will show every reader how to develop self-leadership, set goals, create learning opportunities, take risks, build a team, sell ideas, and work both within and outside the larger organization. This book is about managing up—about employees taking ownership of their jobs, whether it's an assistant working for a manager or a VP working for the CEO. Softback, 229 pages.

To order, visit www.nelson-motivation.com or call 800-575-5521